Christ as the Reality

Witness Lee

Living Stream Ministry
Anaheim, California

First Edition, 3,500 copies. September 1981.
Second Edition, 500 copies. March 1991.
Third Edition, 1,000 copies. October 1996.

ISBN 0-87083-047-3

Published by

Living Stream Ministry
1853 W. Ball Road, Anaheim, CA 92804 U.S.A.
P. O. Box 2121, Anaheim, CA 92814 U.S.A.
Printed in the United States of America

CONTENTS

PREFACE

This book is composed of messages given by Brother Witness Lee in the spring of 1971 in Los Angeles, California.

CHAPTER ONE

THE TENT OF MEETING
AND ALL THE OFFERINGS

Scripture Reading: Gen. 1:1, 26-27; 50:26; Exo. 1:1; 40:34, 38; Lev. 1:1-17; 6:8-13; Heb. 10:5-7; 9:14a; Phil. 2:7-8

The first important matter in regard to seeing Christ as the reality is to realize that Christ is the reality by which we worship God. In the universe, the relationship between man and God is man's worship to God. Whatever we are, whatever we do, and whatever we work must all be for the worship to God. So when we mention worship to God, it includes all these things.

To take Christ as our reality means to take Christ as our being, our doing, our living, and even as our worship to God. I believe that we know something of Christ as reality in a general way, but we are not so clear concerning Christ as reality in details. This has been buried in the Bible for centuries. Although it is in the Bible, it has never been adequately discovered and unveiled. But I believe that in these last days this very thing has been more and more opened up to us. It has been more than ever before discovered and unveiled. So we need to spend some time to see Christ in the pages of the Old Testament as well as the New Testament. The New Testament is so simple and brief, while the Old Testament gives us a picture in detail. Just in the one book of Leviticus, we can see all the details of Christ as the reality to us by which we worship God.

THE SITUATION IN GENESIS AND EXODUS

In the above verses, we have read both the first and last

verses of Genesis and Exodus before coming to Leviticus. This is quite meaningful. In the beginning God created the heavens and the earth, and of course, God created man. Man was created by God to express God Himself and to represent God for His dominion. Man was the center of God's creation to express Him and to represent Him. But at the end of the book of Genesis, we see that the man created by God died and was put into a coffin in Egypt. How poor and pitiful! If this were the end of the Scriptures, we all would be finished. But this is not the ultimate consummation. After Genesis, there is Exodus. There is a way out, an exit—praise the Lord! But the beginning of Exodus is not as glorious as the beginning of Genesis. At the beginning of Genesis, God created the heavens, the earth, and man. This is wonderful. But man fell, died, and was put into a coffin in Egypt. Then Exodus begins with all of the children of Israel in Egypt. Everyone, without exception, was in Egypt. How poor! But how glorious when we reach the end of Exodus. Instead of a coffin, there is a tabernacle. Instead of a dead corpse, there is the shekinah glory of God. The coffin was individualistic, while the tabernacle is corporate. Whenever there are the words, "the tabernacle of the congregation" or "the tent of the congregation," we should read "the tent of meeting." I really like this term "meeting." It is not a tent of individuals, but a tent of meeting.

GOD ON THE EARTH

In Exodus there was a tent of meeting for God's dwelling. He was no longer just in the heavens; He was also on the earth in the tent of meeting. When we come to the book of Leviticus, we find that God speaks out of the tent of meeting. On Mount Sinai, God spoke from the heavens, but since God has a tent of meeting on the earth, He can speak out of it. This is marvelous! Out of all the coffins, God raised up a people and brought them out of Egypt to build them together to become the tent of meeting.

Where were we before we were saved? We were just in a coffin. And we were not in a corporate coffin, but in so many separate and individualistic coffins in the world. All the young brothers and sisters and all the older ones were in the same situation. We were all "in a coffin in Egypt." But, hallelujah, the day came when the Lord called us out of the coffins and brought us out of the world! We had a real exodus. And now He has brought us together in the tent of meeting. Today we can all declare that there is a tent of meeting in Los Angeles! There is no need for God to speak out of the heavens because He has a tent of meeting. The Lord is speaking today out of the local churches, and the local churches are the tents of meeting.

After God's creation and the fall of man, through His redemption, there is a tent of meeting. This is so marvelous to me! I am so excited because I see the tent of meeting! We should never be disappointed or defeated, because we have the tent of meeting. The tent of meeting is a glorious victory over all the deadening works of Satan. God is so victorious and successful. We should all be excited, and we should excite others. Just look at the people today in the world. Everybody has such a sad face, and they are all so disappointed, but we are so happy and excited. Praise the Lord, today in the city of Los Angeles, in the district of Hollywood, there is a tent of meeting!

THE NEED OF LEVITICUS
AND OUR COOPERATION

After Exodus we need the book of Leviticus, because in the tent of meeting God wants to enjoy Christ as the reality. This is all God is doing in the tent of meeting. He just wants to enjoy Christ as the reality in every aspect. This is why after Exodus, there is the need of Leviticus. Leviticus tells us how God enjoys Christ as everything in the tent of meeting.

How can God enjoy Christ? It must be by our cooperation. If God has a tent of meeting on the earth and Christ is everything to God as reality, yet there is no man to offer Christ to God, this means that there is no human cooperation. Let me illustrate it in this way: Suppose there is a kitchen stocked with abundant food. What then do we need? A cook! But God is not the cook—we are! We must cook the food, and eventually God will come to be the co-eater with us. Generally, in the family, only the wives cook. The husbands, then, are the co-eaters with their wives. This is exactly the same situation with God and man in the tent of meeting.

At the tent of meeting there is no arduous labor, but continual cooking and eating. Leviticus is a book of the church life in the meeting, because it covers all the things related to the tent of meeting. We are the tent of meeting, and we are simply meeting people. We must meet all the time, morning and evening. How wonderful it would be if we could do nothing but meet all the time every day! And in the meeting we just cook and eat. We do the cooking, and God eats with us.

And what is the food for all of our cooking and eating with God? It is Christ! We may say that Leviticus is a book of the church meetings, and we may also call Leviticus a book of recipes. All the wives who cook have a recipe book. Leviticus is a recipe book telling us how to cook Christ. It tells us how to feed and satisfy God by cooking Christ. God is hungry! But praise the Lord that God has raised up the local churches as real kitchens. Now God is waiting for all of us to cook Christ in many ways to satisfy Himself and to satisfy ourselves. We need to read Leviticus again and again. All the things mentioned in this book are about Christ. By this book we can learn how to cook Christ to satisfy God.

THE ENLARGED CHRIST

In Exodus, the tent of meeting, the tabernacle, which is just the enlarged Christ, was set up. In the tabernacle, the ark is the center and the content, and the ark is just

Christ Himself. The ark is the vessel that contains the Ten Commandments of God, and the Ten Commandments are the very expression and representation of God. This means that the ark contains God as the content to be expressed. The ark is composed of two kinds of materials: wood overlaid with gold. Gold and wood typify the two natures, the divine nature and the human nature. This is Christ. Christ is of both the divine and human natures. He contains God within Himself as the very center and content of the tabernacle.

The tabernacle is a larger vessel, also made of two main materials—wood overlaid with gold. This reveals that the tabernacle is just the enlargement of the ark, the increase of the ark. When the ark is enlarged, it is the tabernacle. This means that when Christ is enlarged, He becomes the church. The church is just the enlargement of Christ. Strictly speaking, the church is also Christ (1 Cor. 12:12). The ark is the individual Christ, and the tabernacle is the corporate Christ. Praise the Lord that we have Christ enlarged on the earth as the tent of meeting, and in this tent of meeting there is the dwelling of God. God dwells in the enlarged Christ, and God speaks out of the enlarged Christ. We need to realize that this enlarged Christ includes all of us. We are the increase of Christ, so we are the tent of meeting. The tent of meeting is just the enlarged Christ in a corporate way.

TABERNACLED AMONG US

The tent of meeting brings God to the earth. God is no longer in the heavens; He is here in the tent of meeting. Christ enlarged as the tent of meeting brings God to the earth. "In the beginning was the Word, and the Word was with God and the Word was God...And the Word was made flesh, and dwelt among us" (John 1:1, 14). The word "dwelt" in Greek means "tabernacled." The Word became flesh and tabernacled among us. He as the Word was God, and one day this Word became flesh to tabernacle among

us and bring God from heaven to earth in the tent of
meeting. Today God is in the tent of meeting. This is
clearly seen in 1 Corinthians 14 where people coming into
the tent of meeting of the local church say "that God is
among you indeed" (v. 25, ASV). God today is in the tent
of meeting, and this tent of meeting is just Christ
enlarged. Christ enlarged brings God to the earth.

CHRIST
AS THE OFFERINGS

But this is only one part. Christ is not only the tent
of meeting; He is also all the offerings. He is the
tabernacle, and He is also all the offerings. The tabernacle
brings God to man, and the offerings bring man to God.
This is not one-way traffic, but coming and going in two
ways. Christ comes as the tabernacle, and Christ goes as
the offering. Christ comes to us with *God,* and Christ
goes back to God with *us.* In other words, by His coming
He brings God to us, and by His going He brings us to
God.

We are sinful, but Christ as the tabernacle has brought
God to us. We also need Christ as the offerings to bring
us to God. The shekinah glory of God is in the tent of
meeting, but how can we approach it? We need the
offerings. Christ as the offerings brings us to God.

As the tabernacle, Christ is the means by which God
is joined to us. However, the tabernacle cannot be mingled
with us, but only joined to us. But Christ as the offerings
can be mingled with us. All the offerings are to be eaten
and assimilated by us. By assimilation, the food is mingled with us. The offerings are so that Christ can
be mingled with us. By this we have more subjective
experiences of Christ. Christ is not merely joined to us,
but mingled and blended with us. He said in John 6:57,
"he who eats Me shall also live because of Me." We become
what we eat. After eating a chicken, the chicken becomes
a part of us. In Leviticus, nearly all the offerings are
good for eating. Whatever we offer to God is God's food

as well as our food. This is the way that Christ brings us
to God.

A PRESENT TO GOD

God is now in the tent of meeting, but we need to
present Christ as all the offerings that we may contact
God. The word "offer" according to Darby's New Translation should be "present." We need to present Christ to
God as all kinds of presents. Christ as the offering is a
kind of present to God. We need to present to God
the burnt offering present, the meal offering present, the
peace offering present, the sin offering present, and
the trespass offering present.

However, if we are going to present something, we
must first possess it. We must pay the price and get
whatever we need in a proper way. This is our problem.
Many times we come to the meetings without any present
for God. This is why we need to labor on Christ all the
day long in order to have some good produce. Then we
can bring something to present to God as a present. It
is not that God is demanding something from us. He only
desires that we would give Him a present of Christ. If
we are only fulfilling a demand, it is not so pleasing, but
if we offer a present, how sweet and pleasant it is to
God. God has no requirements for us in the tent of
meeting. He only wants us to present Him with something
of Christ. Christ is the only present that God desires.

Today God is seeking the true worshippers who
worship Him in spirit and in reality (John 4:24). Christ
is the reality of all the presents that we must present to
Him. Therefore, we must feed on Christ all the time. We
must eat Him in order to have Him mingled with us.
Then we are one with Christ, and He becomes the very
present that we present to God. This will satisfy God and
it will also satisfy us. Then we will see the richness and
the fullness of the tent of meeting. This is exactly what
the church life in the meetings should be like.

CHAPTER TWO

GOD'S REQUIREMENTS AND GOD'S FOOD

Scripture Reading: Lev. 1:1-10, 14-17; 6:8-13; 7:8; Psa. 20:3; Num. 28:2

Note: In order to be more accurate according to the original language, changes should be made in the above verses. Change all the instances of "bring" to the verb "present" except in Leviticus 1:15; "the priest shall bring it unto the altar." Also change "offer" to "present." The word "offerings" should be changed to the noun "present," except when it reads "burnt offering." Also in the phrase "an offering by fire," it should remain as "offering." "Burnt sacrifice" should also be changed to "burnt offering."

We have seen two things whereby God meets us and we meet God. It is by the tabernacle that God comes to meet us, and it is by the offerings that we can meet God. This is Christ coming and going. God is in the heavens, and we are on the earth. How can God come to us? Praise the Lord, it is through Christ being the tabernacle! And how can we go to God? It is by Christ being all the offerings.

THE REQUIREMENTS OF GOD

Exodus shows us a tabernacle on the earth, and this tabernacle is of three parts. There is the outer court, which has a white linen fence enclosing the tabernacle. Then within the outer court, there is the tabernacle which is divided into two parts: the holy place, which is the outer part and the Holy of Holies, which is the inner part. Within the Holy of Holies, there is the ark. These three parts comprise the tent of meeting, which is Christ enlarged.

Christ Himself is the ark individually, and when He is enlarged, He becomes the tabernacle. This signifies the church; so it is called the tent of meeting.

Once the tabernacle is erected, God is no more just the God in the heavens, but the very God on the earth among His people. Christ as the tabernacle has brought God down to the earth. God is now in the tent of meeting, in the midst of us, through Christ the tabernacle. God is here, but how may we contact Him? God is on the earth among the people, but look at ourselves. We are so sinful. How can we contact God? This is the reason for the fence in the outer court. The white linen fence signifies the righteousness of God. God is righteous, and His righteousness is an enclosing fence. If we would contact this very God who is now on the earth among His people, we need to pass through this fence. In other words, we must meet the requirements of this fence. The righteousness of God is a kind of requirement.

Can we meet the righteous requirement of God? In ourselves, we are nothing but sin and unrighteousness. We are not qualified to meet the requirement of God's righteousness. But praise the Lord, we have Christ! Christ is God's righteousness; so He is qualified to meet the requirement on our behalf.

Within the tabernacle, on nearly every side, there is gold. All the boards on each of the four sides are overlaid with gold. It is a golden place. Gold signifies God's nature, which is holy. Not only is the righteousness of God a requirement, but also His holiness. If we would meet with God, we must meet the requirement of His holiness as well as His righteousness.

In addition, on the ceiling at the top of the tabernacle there are the cherubim. The cherubim in typology signify God's glory. Thus, there is another requirement, the requirement of God's glory. If we would meet with God, we must meet these three divine requirements. There is the requirement of divine righteousness, divine holiness, and divine glory. God is now on the earth in the tabernacle, but do not think that He is on the earth in a careless way. He is enclosed by His righteousness and holiness, and He is also covered by His glory.

There is the separating line of white linen. This is the first enclosure of the righteousness of God. God's righteousness is a separating line. It separates unrighteousness from righteousness. The second enclosure is made of gold. Linen is the first boundary, and gold is the second. Righteousness is the first requirement, and holiness is the second. God is enclosed within these two requirements, and He is covered by His glory. If we would enter the Holy of Holies to meet this righteous, holy, and glorious God, we need to meet all His requirements. Do you think that you can make it? Do you have the righteousness, the holiness, and the glory? We need Christ not only as the tabernacle, but also as the offerings.

THE NEED OF CHRIST
AS THE OFFERINGS

Christ has brought God down to the earth by being the tabernacle, but without Christ as the offerings, we simply cannot meet the requirements of God. Hallelujah, Christ is all kinds of offerings! In all these offerings, Christ meets the requirements of the white linen, the gold, and the cherubim. Christ as the offerings is capable, qualified, and equipped to meet all the requirements of the divine righteousness, holiness, and glory. Praise the Lord that we have Christ! And who is Christ? Christ is the righteousness of God, Christ is the holiness of God, and Christ is the glory of God. When we have Christ, we have these three attributes of God. Then we are able to meet all of God's requirements. But it is not in ourselves; it is in Christ and by Christ. Hallelujah, Christ is our righteousness! Christ is our holiness! Christ is our glory! Whatever God requires, we have, because we have Christ. Therefore, we can walk into the tent of meeting with peace and joy to meet God.

On the one hand Christ is the tabernacle for God to come to us, and on the other hand Christ is the offerings for us to go to God. He is the way for God to come to man, and He is also the way for man to go to God. Eventually, He is the very tent of meeting. Here we meet not only with one another, but also with God. This is because Christ has brought God to us, and Christ brings us to God.

OUR FIRST SITUATION BEFORE GOD

The Burnt Offering

In the book of Leviticus, we see that Christ is typified by many different kinds of offerings. If we read through the first six or seven chapters of this book, we see at least five main offerings: the burnt offering, the meal offering, the peace offering, the sin offering, and the trespass offering. Accompanying these five, there are the wave offering and the heave offering. Why do we need so many kinds of offerings? It is because we are in a situation of at least five to seven aspects before God.

Our first situation is that we are not for God. Of course, before we were saved, we were absolutely not for God. Now that we are saved, in a sense we are for God, but in another sense, we are still not for God. Are you absolutely for God? This is the first aspect of our situation. Whether we are good or whether we are bad, whether we are doing right or doing wrong, the pitiful thing is that we are not really for God. You may be doing good and still not be for God, just as others may be doing bad and not be for God. Regardless of whether we are good or bad, we are altogether not for God. One person may be a bank robber, and another may be a gentleman, but both are not for God. Therefore, in a sense, all are the same, whether they are robbers or college professors. Sometimes even the Christian teachers, preachers, and pastors are not for God. Your reading of the Bible may not be for God, just as reading a magazine may not be for God.

A Man for God

Do you really care absolutely for God? Can you say that whatever you do, whatever you say, and whatever you are is one hundred percent for God? No, none of us can honestly say this. Then what shall we do? We must take Christ! We need Him as our burnt offering. The burnt offering signifies that Christ is the One who is absolutely for God. If you would read the four Gospels again, you would see a Man living on the earth who was one hundred percent for God. Whatever He was, whatever He spoke, and whatever He did was absolutely for God. On the contrary, we are not for God. We are for our own interests and our own choices. But Christ as our burnt offering is completely for God.

In the past, my realization was that we need Christ first of all as our trespass offering. But today my realization has changed. We need Christ first as our burnt offering, because our first problem with God is not a matter of trespasses, but a matter of not being for God. Whether we have trespassed or not, we are still not much for God. We may have done nothing amiss, but we are still not for God. Though I may not be wrong with this person or that person, I am wrong with God because I am still not absolutely for Him. So our first need is Christ as the burnt offering.

Food for God

I was a Christian for years before I realized that God needs food. I was not aware that God is hungry. Then one day I read Numbers 28:2, which says that the burnt offering is the bread of God. The burnt offering is food for God. God is hungry; God needs something to satisfy Himself, and this something is the burnt offering offered by His people. Do you satisfy God day by day? God commanded the children of Israel to present the burnt offering every day both in the morning and in the evening. God needs this kind of food. Many Christians may talk about glorifying God, but God would reply that He is hungry. He needs food. You may say that you will go to the mission field to glorify God, but God would say that He desires food from you today right where you are. How can we know that we are offering food to God? It is when we are satisfied. When we are satisfied, surely God is satisfied by the food we offer Him. If God is not satisfied, we can never be satisfied. So many missionaries are working day and night on the mission field, but are not satisfied. If they would be honest, they would say that although they are doing much work to glorify God, yet they are so hungry. That is a strong proof that God is also hungry. God needs food, and that food is just the burnt offering. We must be absolutely for God. When we offer Christ as our burnt offering, we have the deep conviction that we are satisfied, and our satisfaction is just a proof of God's satisfaction.

The Life for Self
and the Life for God

We must be clear which life is the life that is absolutely for God. Our life is just the life for self; it is not a life for God. Regardless of how much we train ourselves to be for God, eventually we will be just for ourselves. In principle it is similar to a monkey which has been trained to eat like a man. Regardless of how much you train him to eat food in a human way, eventually the monkey will revert to his own way, because he has only the monkey life. How can a monkey behave like a human if he does not have the human life? In the same way, our life is a life for self and not for God.

I have heard others saying that a certain person is self-centered. You may say that that person is self-centered, but I will ask, "What about you?" I am not worried about that person being self-centered. I am the same. In a sense, we may be more self-centered than the person of whom we are speaking. Suppose I ask the wives if their husbands are self-centered. If they say that their husbands are self-centered, then I would ask whether the wives are self-centered. We are all self-centered. There is no need to condemn others for being self-centered; we are all the same.

But hallelujah! There is another life we can experience. We can be one with Him; we can rely upon Him. We can be one with Christ as our burnt offering. He is the life in us which is absolutely for God. Our life may be self-centered, but His life is God-centered.

The Handling
of the Burnt Offering

According to the record of Leviticus 1, those who present the burnt offering must kill it, flay or skin it, and cut it into pieces. Then they must wash all the inward parts and the legs with all the other parts that must be burnt. But we must realize that we are unable to kill, to skin, and to cut into pieces. Our life is unable to do this. The life for killing, for flaying, for cutting, and for washing is altogether Christ. Do you think that you can cut yourself into pieces? You cannot! There is only one life which is able to do this, and that is Christ.

The Practical Application

If only you will stay in your spirit where you are one with Christ, there will be some killing, some flaying, some cutting into pieces, and some washing. There will even be some burning. If we are one with Christ in the spirit, we will experience the killing, the flaying, the cutting, the washing, and eventually the burning until we become ashes. When we become ashes, it is a strong proof that God has accepted our present.

Psalm 20:3 says, "Remember all thy offerings, and accept thy burnt offering." The notes of some versions indicate that the word "accept" in this verse in the original language means "turn to ashes." When God turns our burnt offering to ashes, that means that He has accepted our burnt offering. The note in the ASV says that the word "accept" in Hebrew means "accept as fat." In Hebrew the word for "ashes" is the same word for "fat." In our eyes it is ashes, but to God it is fat. It is ashes, but God accepts it as fat. It pleases and satisfies God as fat. The more we become ashes, the more we are nothing, the more we become fat to God. This is something sweet to God, and this is the way that God accepts our burnt offering. How do we know that God accepts our present as a sweet burnt offering? It is when we realize that we have become nothing but ashes.

We ourselves should not attempt to be burnt. No matter how much you try to be burnt, you will escape. The more you try to be nothing but ashes, the more you will be something. Do not try to be burnt; do not try to become ashes. Just stay in the spirit, taking Christ as your burnt offering. Then there will be the killing, the flaying, the cutting, the washing, the burning, and eventually the ashes. Whenever we come to the meeting, we must come with such a Christ as the burnt offering for us to present to God. This is food to God. This is Christ as reality in our worship to God.

I do look to the Lord that He will bring us all into the reality of experiencing Christ as the burnt offering in such a way. We need to enjoy Christ in such a way that when the killing, the flaying, the cutting, the washing, and the burning comes, we will be one with Christ, so willing to take all these things. It is not by trying to take them by ourselves, but by being one with Christ. We need these kinds of deeper experiences. Then the meetings, full of such a Christ, will be a real enjoyment to God.

The Covering of Christ

There is one more point concerning the burnt offering: the priests and those who present the burnt offering are not allowed to eat any part of it; it is absolutely for God. But the skin is for the priest who presents the burnt offering. If we present the burnt offering, it will be burnt to ashes for God, yet the skin will be ours. This means that the more we present Christ as our burnt offering, the more we will be covered by Him. God enjoys Christ as the burnt offering, and this Christ becomes our covering. In other words, the more we offer Christ as the burnt offering to God, the more we will be in Christ. We will simply be covered by Christ. A person may say that he is in Christ, but many times it is rather difficult to see Christ upon him. But the more he experiences Christ as the burnt offering, and presents Him to God in the tent of meeting, the more he is covered with Christ. He is under the covering of Christ, and he shares this covering. God shares the enjoyment, and he shares the covering because the skin is his.

We need to bring these points to the Lord and pray. We need to pray-read these verses in Leviticus 1 concerning the burnt offering a few more times. Then the Lord will point out something to us. We are not here for the teaching of typology or for any doctrine. We are here for something deeper of Christ as the reality. This is the way not only to experience Christ as the reality, but also to enjoy Him as our reality. Then in the meetings there will be so many who can present Christ as the burnt offering to God and share the covering of Christ.

CHAPTER THREE

EIGHT POINTS
OF THE BURNT OFFERING

Scripture Reading: Deut. 12:8-14; Lev. 1:3, 7-10, 14, 16; 2 Cor. 4:10-12, 16

God needs food to satisfy His hunger, and the burnt offering according to divine revelation is not just a kind of sacrifice, but food for God. Leviticus 3:11, speaking of the burnt offering, says, "And the priest shall burn it upon the altar: it is the food of the offering made by fire unto the Lord." This verse, along with Leviticus 21:6, 8, 21, and 22, shows us that the burnt offering is food for God. God is hungry and needs to be satisfied. So we must provide the burnt offering for His food.

All the different offerings are not only for our enjoyment, but also for God's enjoyment. They are a kind of mutual enjoyment. God enjoys all the offerings, and we enjoy them too. All the offerings are types of the different aspects of Christ. Christ is so rich; He has so many aspects. Such a rich Christ is a mutual enjoyment both to God and to us. Thus, Leviticus is not merely a book of law, but a book of enjoyment.

The first offering, which is the burnt offering, is for God's enjoyment. There is only a small portion for our enjoyment, that is, the skin for the priest who presents the burnt offering to God. Most of the burnt offering is for God's food, but still there is a small part for our covering. The burnt offering is not for us to eat, but to put on. It is God's enjoyment, but it is our covering. We have no right to enjoy Christ as the burnt offering for our food; it is God's food. But there is a little part for our covering. The more we present Christ as enjoyment to God, the more we are in Christ and covered with Him. The more Christ becomes God's enjoyment through our presentation, the more Christ becomes our covering. Eventually, all that others can see of us is Christ. The skin of the burnt offering has become our covering, and we have become one with the burnt offering.

FOOD FOR GOD

There are eight points that we must see concerning the burnt offering. The first is that God is waiting for His food in the tent of meeting. God does not purchase the food, nor does He grow the food by Himself. God is in the tent of meeting, waiting for His food. If there is no one to labor on the good land and no one to present the surplus of the riches of the land in the tent of meeting, there is no way for God to obtain His food. How much God depends upon us and our labor on the good land! He is depending on our presentation of the surplus of the riches of the good land for His food.

We must realize that God has been hungry for centuries because many Christians have not known how to labor on Christ as the good land. They simply have not known that whenever they meet, they should bring something of Christ to God. They have known how to have a so-called Christian service, but they have not known how to bring the surplus of the riches of Christ to God as the burnt offering. They have known how to fast and cry to God for His mercy. Their prayers were mainly, "O God be merciful to us and send a great revival." They simply have not known how to bring the riches of Christ to God as His food.

But praise the Lord that in these last few years He has shown us this very thing. We no longer need to meet in that poor way of fasting, crying, and weeping. We may meet in a joyful way, coming together with the very Christ whom we experience day by day. We have a surplus of this rich Christ, because we have been laboring on Him as the good land all day long. Why do we have the morning watch? Just for laboring on Christ! Why do we call on the name of the Lord? Just to labor on Him! Why do we feast on Him in the Word all the day? Simply for laboring on Him! Christ is our good land, and we labor on Him all the day. Then when we come to the meeting in the tent of meeting, we have something of Christ to present to God. God is really hungry. He is looking forward to the meetings to receive some food. Our meeting together is not just to set up a table among ourselves, but to set up a table for God.

Many Christians are always trying to get something from God. However, in the tent of meeting, the first thing which we must present is the burnt offering, not for our enjoyment, but for God's enjoyment. We must satisfy God with the very Christ upon whom we have labored. This is far from the concept of most Christians. They are always looking to God for something, but they never have anything to present to God as food. We must labor on Christ that we may have something of His surplus to bring to God when we come to the tent of meeting. We can then present the burnt offering to Him for His food.

**DIFFERENT SIZES
OF THE BURNT OFFERING**

The second point is that the burnt offering is in different sizes. There is the bullock which is quite large, the sheep and the goats which are smaller, and then eventually the turtledove or young pigeon which is the smallest. Christ in Himself is always the same. He is unlimitedly great, but He differs in our experience. Sometimes in our experience He is a bullock, and sometimes He is just a little pigeon. Then sometimes He is a sheep—something of medium size. In Himself He is always the same, but in our experiences He differs.

What size Christ have you experienced today? Did you experience Him as a bullock or as a pigeon? We must check to see what is the size of the Christ we have experienced and have brought to present to God in the tent of meeting. Deep within we all know just how large the Christ is whom we have experienced. So we need to pray, "Lord, be gracious to us that we may enlarge our experience of Christ and always have a bullock to present to You."

FOUR MAIN THINGS FOR PRESENTING THE BURNT OFFERING

Third, we must see that to present the burnt offering or even to present all the other offerings, we need four things. We need these four things in order to present the Christ whom we have experienced to God in a proper way. Without them it would be rather difficult for us to present any offerings.

The Unique Place of God's Choice

The first of the four things is the unique place of God's choice. In Deuteronomy 12:8-14, Moses told the people of Israel about the place of God's choice. "Ye shall not do after all the things that we do here this day, every man whatsoever is right in his own eyes. For ye are not as yet come to the rest and to the inheritance, which the Lord your God giveth you. But when ye go over Jordan, and dwell in the land which the Lord your God giveth you to inherit, and when he giveth you rest from all your enemies round about, so that ye dwell in safety; then there shall be a place which the Lord your God shall choose to cause his name to dwell there; thither shall ye bring all that I command you; your burnt offerings, and your sacrifices, your tithes, and the heave offering of your hand, and all your choice vows which ye vow unto the Lord: and ye shall rejoice before the Lord your God, ye, and your sons, and your daughters, and your menservants, and your maid-servants, and the Levite that is within your gates; forasmuch as he hath no part nor inheritance with you.

Take heed to thyself that thou offer not thy burnt offerings in every place that thou seest: but in the place which the Lord shall choose in one of thy tribes, there thou shalt offer thy burnt offerings, and there thou shalt do all that I command thee."

Moses told the people of Israel that when they entered the good land, they should not do things which were right in their own eyes, but not right in the eyes of God. In the wilderness they did whatever was right in their own eyes. That was lawlessness; it was something which could never please God. He tolerated it in the wilderness, but He would not tolerate it in the good land. Then Moses told them that when they entered into the good land, they must present their burnt offerings in the very place of God's choice. If it was according to their choice, it would again be something which was right in their own eyes. But in the good land, they must do what is right in the eyes of God. The first thing they must do is to bring their offerings to the place of God's choice.

This means that when we are not living in Christ, not resting in Christ, and not inheriting our portion in Christ, we may act in a loose way according to our choice. But once we are resting in Christ, inheriting Him as our portion, we should not do things according to our eyes, but according to the choice of God. Praise the Lord that we are now in Christ! We are in the good land! Therefore, we should not do anything according to our choice, but according to God's choice. Thus, for the presenting of the offerings there is the need of a proper place, a place which will keep the unity of the people of God. If the people of Israel had the liberty to choose a place for their worship to God when they went into the good land, it would not be long before they would be divided. Through all the centuries the people of Israel have been kept as one as far as their worship to God is concerned. The unity has been kept by this unique place of worship. The only choice was God's choice, and God's choice was their choice.

Today, Christians are too free; they have too many

choices. Almost everybody has a certain kind of church according to his or her choice. People say, "I don't like that kind of meeting," or "I prefer this kind of meeting." What is this? This is their choice. We all need to say, "Lord, what is *Your* choice? Where is the place *You* have chosen? I do not like my choice. I do not like to do anything that is right in my own eyes, but everything that is right in *Your* eyes. I do not like to meet according to my taste; I want to meet in the place of *Your* choice."

The choices today are too many. You have your taste and I have mine. We all have our own taste; eventually, many tastes cause many divisions. But there is only one proper taste and one proper choice; that is God's choice of the one unique ground of unity. Do not think that this is a small matter. You may see the enjoyment in our meetings and even taste something of that enjoyment, but do not try to go to your place to copy the same thing. You may have the enjoyment here, but if you go to other places to copy these things, you will immediately lose the enjoyment. This is because you are not in the one unique place chosen by God, that is, the genuine ground of unity. We all need to be on the unique ground of unity. Do not meet with the local church because it suits your taste. Whether you like it or not does not matter. What matters is whether or not God likes it. While you say that you like it tonight, tomorrow you may not like it. We must say that this is God's choice, and God's choice is our destiny. It is not a small thing to be in the place of God's choice on the ground of unity. Hundreds of us can testify that as long as we are on the ground of unity, we are home. We are home because this is God's choice.

The Tent of Meeting

The second of the four things which we need in order to properly present the offerings to God is the tent of meeting. What is the tent of meeting? This is the meeting of the local church. Without the church meetings, how could we present the burnt offering to God as His food?

We all need the church meetings. If you do not believe it, just try to offer Christ as the burnt offering to God in your home by yourself. It will not work. Some may say, "Brother Lee, you are too narrow. You are limiting God. If I can present Christ as the burnt offering to God in the meeting, I can surely do it in my home!" All I can say is that those who feel this way should go home and try to do it.

According to the type, the picture is very clear. Not one Israelite was allowed to present the burnt offering in his home. Have you read this? Today, so many Christians say that they do not care for the meetings. As long as they are fellowshipping with the Lord in their home or somewhere else, they feel that it is all right. In a sense, it is all right, but it is not all right for offering Christ as the burnt offering to God. No Israelite in ancient times could kill a bullock for a burnt offering to God in any place he chose. He had to be at the tent of meeting. Only at the door of the tent of meeting was he able to present the burnt offering. You may enjoy Christ in your home tonight, and you may enjoy Christ in your home tomorrow morning, and you may enjoy Christ anytime in any place, but you can never present Christ as the burnt offering to God for God's food in any place other than the meeting of the local church.

In the meetings we have a certain kind of sensation that is so sweet and pleasant. There is the sensation that something here is so unique, so pleasant, and so good. Try to imitate this sensation at home. You simply cannot do it. You can never have such a sensation outside of the tent of meeting. We all must come to the church meetings to present our burnt offering to God. In the church meetings we sense something of Christ which we can never sense in any other place. Leviticus 1:3 says clearly that we must present our burnt offering at the door of the tent of meeting before the Lord. This is the only place to present Christ as the burnt offering. You may try to do it according to Matthew 18:20: "For where two or three are gathered together in My name, there I am in their midst." However, I know that many of us have tried this already and have no desire to try it again. Praise the Lord that today we are on the unique ground, and we do have the tent of meeting where we can offer our burnt offering to God as food!

The Altar

The third item is the altar. In the Old Testament times there was only one altar among the people of Israel. There were no altars in the homes. The altar was unique, because it was in the unique place that God chose. As long as there is only one altar, how can we present the burnt offering in our home? The altar is at the tent of meeting, not in your home or my home. There is one altar, and we need the altar to present all the offerings, especially the burnt offering.

The Priests

The fourth thing which we must have to properly present the offerings to God is the priests. Praise the Lord, we all may say that we are priests! But we must realize that according to the type, none of the priests was individualistic. All the priests were coordinated into one body. There was one priesthood. The word "priesthood" here means a body of priests. We need the coordination of the body of priests, the priesthood, in order to properly present the burnt offering to God.

Thus, we see four things which we must have to present the burnt offering. We need the unique place, the tent of meeting, the altar, and the priesthood. It is impossible to have these four things in our home. I tried this forty years ago, but it did not work. Then I came to the unique ground of the tent of meeting with the unique altar and the priesthood. It was so easy to present Christ as the burnt offering in the proper place. These four things are the third point we must see in order to present the burnt offering.

IDENTIFIED WITH CHRIST

The fourth point is that in presenting the burnt offering, we are one with Christ. On the one hand the burnt offering is just Christ Himself. Yet, on the other hand, if we would present Christ as the burnt offering, we must be one with Him. This is why in the presentation of the burnt offering there is the laying on of the hand of the presenter. This simply means that the presenter is one with the present; the offerer is one with the offering. To lay your hand upon the head of the burnt offering means to be identified with the offering.

If, throughout the whole day, we have never been one with Christ, it is rather difficult to come into the meeting to present Christ as the burnt offering. If our hand has been kept away from Christ, yet we come to the meeting and try to present Him as our burnt offering, it is indeed awkward. We all must be identified with Christ. We must be one with Christ all day long. All day our hand must be on the head of Christ. In other words, throughout the day we must be one with Christ in our spirit.

This Christ upon whom we lay our hand is not One who kills others. His is not a killing life, but a life that is willing to be killed. Let me illustrate in this way. Here is a brother and his wife. If this brother has really been one with Christ today, he will realize that Christ is not the killing One, but the One who is so willing to be killed. Suppose that when he gets home, his wife gives him a difficult time. This is the killing. Many, many times the wives are the best killers. But I must be fair and say that the husbands are killers, too. The wives are killing the husbands, and the husbands are killing the wives. The lives of both the husbands and of the wives are killing lives. Do not think that a certain brother is so gentle— his life is a cutting life. Many times he cuts his wife into pieces. And his wife has the same kind of life. Perhaps she tries even more to cut him into pieces.

But when your wife or your husband is cutting you into pieces, if you are one with Christ, you will be willing to be cut. The life of Christ within us is so willing to be cut. By His life you will never quarrel; you will never have any exchange of words with your wife. You will be so willing to be cut into pieces. Then when you come to the meeting, you will have something of Christ to offer and present to God. On the other hand, if you quarrel a little with your wife and reason with her in even a small way, you are through. You will come to the meeting with your hands empty. You will have nothing of Christ to offer.

This is the case not only in the marriage life, but also in the office, the classroom, and the apartment where we live. All the time we must experience Christ as the life which is willing to be cut into pieces. It is not by ourselves, but by the indwelling Christ. He is the burnt offering, and His life is so willing to be cut.

Paul says in 2 Corinthians 4:10-12, "Always bearing about in the body the putting to death of Jesus, that the life also of Jesus might be made manifest in our body. For we which live are always delivered unto death for Jesus' sake, that the life also of Jesus might be made manifest in our mortal flesh. So then death worketh in us, but life in you" (lit.). We must bear the putting to death of Jesus in our life. All day long we are given to death.

Do not think that it will be those who are so much against you who will kill you. Many times your wife kills you, and sometimes an elder in the local church kills you. All these are just the proper cuttings for you.

If we are all going to be built up together and have a rich recovery of the church, we all must experience these things. Do not say that when you come to the church the love is so marvelous. After two weeks, you will suffer much. You will suffer the cutting. Do not try to cut others, but be willing to be cut. However, no matter how careful you are, you will sometimes cut others. Many times I was extremely careful not to cut others, but eventually I cut a great deal. I did not do it intentionally, but I did it. We all have cut one another many times, but today we are here in real oneness because we are willing to be cut by one another. We do have a life within us which is willing to be cut.

Do not take this matter of the burnt offering as a teaching in an objective way. We all must realize that the burnt offering is our oneness with Christ. All day long we must identify ourselves with Christ in a practical way in our daily walk. It is not just a matter of coming to the meeting and trying to present Christ as the burnt offering. That will not work. We must be one with Christ in our practical daily lives, and to be one with Christ as the burnt offering means to take the life which is so willing to be killed, skinned, and cut into pieces.

THE ACCEPTANCE OF GOD

Now we come to the fifth point of the burnt offering: when we present Christ as the burnt offering in the tent of meeting, we have the full acceptance of God. If we have been one with Christ during the day, when we come to the meeting we have something to present. When we present Christ as the burnt offering, we have the deep sensation that we are fully accepted by God. We have the full acceptance of God, and we have the full assurance that we are so pleasing to God. When we are identified with Christ in our daily walk and we come to the meeting to present Him as our burnt offering, we are fully assured that God is pleased with us. We have the acceptance of God.

ARRANGED IN ORDER UPON THE FIRE

The sixth point of the burnt offering is the order. In Leviticus 1:7-8, the words "in order" are used twice. "And the sons of Aaron the priest shall put fire upon the altar, and lay the wood in order upon the fire: and the priests, Aaron's sons, shall lay the parts, the head, and the fat, in order upon the wood that is on the fire which is upon the altar." The wood is laid in order, and the pieces of the burnt offering are also laid in order. Nothing is done in a sloppy way. One version says that the wood is arranged. The wood is not thrown upon the altar, but arranged in order, and the pieces of the burnt offering are also laid in an arrangement. What does this mean? God knows which piece of wood is needed for burning your offering. He arranges the wood in a good order. He uses the first piece of wood, the second piece, and then the third piece to burn your offering. God knows also which part of your offering to burn. He arranges the wood, and He arranges the pieces in order. In our experience and to our sensation, the burning might be a mess, but God is a good Arranger. He arranges the burning in a good order. The priest arranged all the pieces of wood in order, and he arranged all the pieces of the burnt offering. God does the same today. Under His arranging, the first piece of wood is really the first, and the second is really the second. And the first part of the offering that is burnt is really the first part. There is nothing amiss. God could never be mistaken in His burning. He burns our offering in a good order.

BURNED AS INCENSE

The seventh point we must see concerning the burnt offering is that the odor is a kind of incense to God. In Hebrew, the word "burnt" used in this chapter means to burn as incense. The burnt offering is an incense to God. It is not a judgment or a punishment, but a burning of incense. It is not under God's punishment, but under God's acceptance. It is not like the burning of the lake of fire, but the burning on the altar as the burning of the incense altar. It is so sweet and fragrant to God. This is why our meetings are so fragrant. Many of us sense that when we come to the meeting, there is the sweet odor of incense. This is because so many under the sweet burning have Christ as their burnt offerings. It is not a burning as a kind of sore punishment, but a burning as a sweet incense. Thus, there is a sweet fragrance.

If we would be willing to be identified with Christ in our daily walk, whenever we come together and present

Christ as the burnt offering to God, there will be a sweet fragrance in our meetings. No words can explain it. It is not a good speaker attracting the people or a great movement stirring them up. It is just the little ones meeting together with something fragrant. When people come into their midst, they sense the sweetness and the fragrance. This is the burnt offering presented to God through so many dear ones who are one with Christ in their daily life.

THE ASHES ON THE EAST

Finally, the last point regarding the burnt offering is the ashes on the east (Lev. 1:16). The ashes mean the remainder of the dead and burnt body. It was a living body, but it was killed and burnt to ashes. Humanly speaking, when any living one becomes ashes, that is the end, the real termination. But with Christ as the burnt offering, the ashes are not the end, but just the beginning. The ashes were not put at the sunset on the west, but at the place of the sunrise on the east. Assuredly the sun will rise. The ashes mean that Christ has been put to death, but the east signifies resurrection. After the putting to death, resurrection will follow. Paul says that we bear the putting to death of Jesus that the life also of Jesus might be manifested in us. This is resurrection. The more we become ashes with Christ, the more we will be put to the east. And on the east we have assurance that the sun will rise. Hallelujah for the sunrise of resurrection!

CHAPTER FOUR

THE HUMANITY OF JESUS—
THE MEAL OFFERING

Scripture Reading: Lev. 2:1-16 (Note: change the word "meat" to "meal" throughout this chapter.)

We have pointed out that there are five kinds of offerings because we are in five situations before God. Our first situation is that we are not for God; therefore, we need the burnt offering. The burnt offering is Christ who is absolutely for God. Now we come to our second situation before God, that is, we are not perfect and fine. Fine means there is nothing rough or coarse; it also means there is nothing short and nothing too much. Sometimes we are just a little too much in certain things, and sometimes we lack in the things that are necessary. So because we are not perfect and fine, we need the second kind of offering. This is the meal offering made of fine flour.

THE DIFFERENCE BETWEEN THE BURNT OFFERING AND THE MEAL OFFERING

Why does the meal offering follow the burnt offering? To see this we must see the differences between the burnt offering and the meal offering. The burnt offering is something of the animal life: a bullock, a sheep, or a turtledove. But the meal offering is absolutely of another kingdom. It is not of the animal kingdom, but of the vegetable kingdom. Fine flour is made from wheat. The Lord Jesus is pictured as being of two kinds of lives: the animal life and the vegetable life. The animal life is for redeeming, for there is the shedding of blood. Without the shedding of blood, there is no redemption. The vegetable life is for generating or producing.

In the Gospel of John, the Lord is portrayed as having both the animal and the vegetable life. John 1:29 says, "Behold, the Lamb of God Who takes away the sin of the world!" John 12:24 says, "Unless a grain of wheat falls into the ground and dies, it abides alone; but if it dies, it bears much fruit." As the Lamb, He is of the animal kingdom, and as the grain of wheat, He is of the vegetable kingdom. Thus, by these two chapters in John, we realize that the Lamb, the animal life, is for redeeming, and the grain of wheat, the vegetable life, is for producing. One grain produces many grains. The Lord Jesus is the Lamb, and He is also the grain of wheat. He is of the animal life and also of the vegetable life. He is the redeeming One, and He is also the producing One.

By this we see that the burnt offering is mainly for redeeming. In Leviticus 1, the word "blood" is mentioned at least three times. The burnt offering is for our redemption by the sprinkled blood. We are told clearly that the burnt offering is not for our food or satisfaction, but wholly for God's satisfaction. The meal offering, however, is mainly for our nourishment. We need to be redeemed, and we also need to be nourished. The burnt offering satisfies God, but the meal offering not only satisfies God, but also makes us alive. It causes us to live in the presence of God.

Another thing which we must see is that all the sufferings in the burnt offering are for redemption. The sufferings in the meal offering, however, are not for redeeming, but are the personal sufferings. Furthermore, in the burnt offering, the blood is prominent, but with the meal offering, the prominent things are the oil and the frankincense.

THE DIFFERENCE BETWEEN THE MEAL OFFERING AND THE MANNA

Not only do we need to see the difference between the burnt offering and the meal offering, but also between

manna and the meal offering. Many Christians think
that manna is wonderful. But in the book of Leviticus,
the manna is past; it is replaced by something better and
richer. The first difference is that manna is from heaven,
but the meal offering is from the earth. We would think
that something from heaven should be wonderful. Could
anything be better than that which is from heaven? But
the meal offering is of the earth. Manna was *given* from
heaven, but the meal offering was *grown up* from the
earth.

Isaiah 4:2 tells us that the Lord Jesus on the one hand
is "the branch of Jehovah." This speaks of His divinity.
But on the other hand it says that He is "the fruit of the
earth." This is His humanity. As to His divine nature, He
is the branch of Jehovah, and as to His human nature,
He is the fruit of the earth. Isaiah 53 speaks of the Lord
as a "tender plant" grown out of dry ground. He is the
fruit of the earth, and He is a tender plant out of dry
ground. For the meal offering we do not need the divinity
of the Lord Jesus; we need His humanity. His humanity
is for our perfection. It is not something given from heaven,
but grown from the earth. Many Christians would never
think that something of the earth could be better than
something from heaven. But the meal offering is better
than manna.

Also, manna is a gift *from* God, and the meal offering
is a present *to* God. Which is better? We must see that a
present to God is much better. We must be delivered from
our old concepts. Manna is for our satisfaction; it is not
for God's satisfaction. The meal offering, however, is for
God's satisfaction. It is even a memorial to God—this is
something more than satisfaction. "And the priest shall
burn the memorial of it [the meal offering] upon the altar,
to be an offering made by fire, of a sweet savor unto the
Lord" (Lev. 2:2). Manna is not for God's satisfaction, but
the meal offering is for God's satisfaction, and it is a
memorial in His presence. It is something for God to
remember. This is much better.

Moreover, manna is for a life in the wilderness,

whereas the meal offering is for a life in God's dwelling place. Manna is sufficient only to sustain a life in the wilderness, but the meal offering will support a life in the dwelling place of God. Where do you prefer to be: in the wilderness or in the dwelling place of God? We all must prefer to have the meal offering, and we must forget the manna. The meal offering suffices for a life serving God in His presence and in His dwelling place. There is no more wandering, but just dwelling with God in His house.

Another important point of difference between the manna and the meal offering is that manna never constituted worship to God. God never asked His people to worship Him by presenting manna. But God did command His people to worship Him with the meal offering. Thus the meal offering is quite sufficient to constitute worship to God. This is why among many Christians there is really no true worship to God. People are always feeding on manna. In the local churches we must have true worship to God by enjoying the meal offering all the day long.

There is one additional point concerning the manna and the meal offering. With manna, there is no need of human labor. But to have the meal offering, there is much need of human labor. We must labor on the good land by tilling the ground, sowing the seed, watering the plants, and reaping the harvest. We must care for many things in order to obtain the fine flour. Even after the harvest, there is the grinding and the baking. All of this is not done in the tent of meeting, but at home. All that is required for the manna is to go out and gather it. The meal offering requires much more labor than the manna.

So many young people today are loose and careless. Many times I decided to visit the young people's houses, but my wife said that I should call them first. But if I did that, there would be no need to go. My intention was to see how they keep their rooms and their kitchen. So many of them shout, "O Lord, Amen, Hallelujah!" but I want to see their bedroom. I am afraid that many of them did not make their beds today. If that is true, it is certainly not the fine flour. I like to hear the young people shout, "Hallelujah," but "Hallelujah" what? Sometimes I would rather go to their bedroom to see how they labor on Christ and till the ground by making their bed.

Sloppy ones cannot even get the manna. There may not be much labor, but you still must rise early and go out of the camp to gather it. God is merciful, but He is not so gracious if you are sloppy. God will send the manna outside the camp, but He will not send it into your bedroom and into your mouth. You must rise early, get out of your bed, leave your bedroom, and go out of the camp to pick up the manna. Then you must cook it a little before you eat it.

Solomon says in Proverbs 19:24 that the lazy man, even when he stretches out his hand for food, will not take it back. He is really lazy. A lazy person cannot obtain even the manna, not to mention the meal offering. The meal offering requires much more labor than the manna.

THE FINE FLOUR

Now we must see something of the ingredients of the meal offering. As we have mentioned, the main substance is the fine flour, which is derived from the vegetable life. In the Bible, the vegetable life always refers to the Lord's humanity. As a man, the Lord Jesus is so perfect, even as fine flour. Fine flour is perfect in its evenness, its fineness, its tenderness, and in its gentleness, thus revealing the balance and evenness of the Lord's humanity.

Some sisters are a little too emotional, and some brothers are a little too mental. Some sisters are so emotional that it seems they never think at all. Some brothers, on the other hand, think too much. Whenever you talk with them, they turn their eyes—a strong proof that they are exercising their mind. I have seen some brothers who are so cold that they cannot even laugh. This means they are not fine, not balanced, and not even; neither are they tender and gentle.

But the Lord Jesus in His humanity is so fine, so even, so tender, and so gentle. When it was time for joy, He was joyful (John 11:15). When it was time for tears, He wept (John 11:35). As a man He was so finely balanced. Sometimes He was bold in rebuking the evil ones, but He was not rough (Matt. 21:12-13; 23:33). He was still fine and even. This is the fine flour. I do not have adequate utterance to speak about the perfect humanity of Christ. It is better to pray-read the four Gospels once more with this point in view. Then we will see the fineness of all His behavior in His human living.

It is this perfect Christ who constitutes our present to God in the tent of meeting. It is not a gift from God to us, but a present from us to God. When we come to the church meeting, we need to offer such a perfect Christ in His humanity as a kind of present to God. We can say, "Father, here is a dear present for You, and this present is just the man Jesus in His humanity." God will be so pleased to receive such a present.

It is no wonder that God is perfect, but that a man is perfect is an astounding fact. Praise the Lord that upon the earth among the human race there was a man so perfect, so even, so fine, and so tender! He was just like the fine flour. This is the humanity of Jesus. This is Jesus, the man. Nothing could be so dear and precious to God as a present to Him of the humanity of Jesus in the tent of meeting. Our present to God must be the man Jesus whom we appreciate, enjoy, and experience all day long.

**A MEMORIAL AND
A SWEET SAVOR**

In Leviticus 1, we cannot find the word "memorial." But this word is used many times in chapter two concerning the meal offering. Its significance is greater than that of satisfaction. If you are not satisfied with something, you can never have a memorial of it. But when you are exceedingly satisfied with something, it becomes a continual memorial to you. This is the man Jesus, the perfect man, the fine man, presented to God by us. This is the greatest satisfaction to God, and this satisfaction eventually becomes a memorial to God forever. It is for eternity.

Here in Los Angeles we have been enjoying Christ so much, and I believe that as we experience the man Jesus more and more, we will have such a dear present to God in our church meeting. This will become an eternal memorial to God, and even to us. I believe that in eternity, we will still remember the enjoyment that we had of the humanity of Jesus on Elden Avenue in Los Angeles. It is better than satisfaction.

The words "sweet savor" are also used concerning the meal offering unto God. Some versions translate this as "fragrance of rest." It is a sweet odor that causes God to be so restful. If we present the man Jesus from our experience as a real present to God, this will become a sweet odor, a restful fragrance, and a satisfying savor.

THE PRIESTLY DIET

We must realize that the meal offering is mainly for us. Only a handful as a memorial is for God; all the remainder, the major part, is for the priests. "And the remainder of the meal offering shall be Aaron's and his sons'" (Lev. 2:3). This is the diet of the priests. The priests feed on Christ as the meal offering day by day. We are the priests, so we must eat Christ as the meal offering for our priestly diet.

The Lord Jesus said in John 6:57, "He who eats Me shall also live because of Me." If we eat the meal offering, we will live by this offering. We are what we eat. What we eat eventually becomes our being. If day by day we eat Christ as our meal offering, eventually we will become Christ. "For to me to live is Christ" (Phil. 1:21). It is this kind of life which is adequate to serve God in the priesthood.

God does not expect the angels to serve Him as priests. He wants human beings. We must not serve God as angels, but as men. For men to serve God is indeed wonderful, but we need the nourishment. To be in the presence of God serving Him, we need the nourishment. To be in the presence of God serving Him, we need an extraordinary diet. That is Christ as the meal offering. The more we enjoy Christ as such a diet, the more we will be nourished, qualified, strengthened, and supported to serve God in a priestly way. This is why we need to experience such a Jesus daily.

We all need to have a change in our diet. Forget about reading magazines or newspapers. We must spend more time in eating the man Jesus in the four Gospels. The humanity of Jesus will then become our real food and our daily diet. When we come to the meeting, we will be real priests serving God.

THE MINGLING OF THE OIL

With the meal offering there is the fine flour, and there is the oil. We all know that oil signifies the divine Spirit. The fine flour is Christ's humanity, and the oil is the divine Spirit. The oil is poured upon and even mingled with the fine flour. I have been criticized in the past for using the word "mingle" to describe the mingling of divinity with humanity. But eventually I found the word here in Leviticus 2:4-5: "...fine flour unleavened, mingled with oil." The fine flour is mingled with the oil! The humanity is mingled with the divinity. The humanity is flavored, strengthened, and watered by the divine Spirit.

John Darby was one who really knew the Bible. In his New Translation of the Bible, he points out that to mingle is more than to anoint. This word was mistranslated in Psalm 92:10 as "anoint." It should be: "I shall be mingled with fresh oil." We all must be mingled with the Holy Spirit. It is not just to have the Holy Spirit poured upon us, anointing us, but to have the Holy Spirit mingled with us. Christ Jesus was such a Person. When He was on the earth, He was a man fully mingled with the Holy Spirit.

THE FRAGRANCE OF FRANKINCENSE

Not only is there oil with the meal offering, but also frankincense. "And thou shalt put oil upon it, and lay frankincense thereon: it is a meal offering" (Lev. 2:15). The frankincense signifies the sweet fragrance of the manifestation of resurrection. When the Lord was on earth, whatever He did in all His activities, behavior, and conversation was always a sweet, fragrant manifestation. His deeds were not natural, but something of resurrection. Though He was not yet crucified, He was living in resurrection. Even when He was twelve, He was in the temple caring for God, behaving Himself in the way of resurrection. He never did anything according to His natural concept; He was always in the manifestation of resurrection life. It was so sweet and so fragrant. He had the real frankincense. In the Lord's humanity, there is always the oil plus the frankincense. There is always the divine Spirit plus the fragrance of resurrection.

One day while He was speaking, He was told that His mother and brothers were looking for Him. He replied that all those who do the will of God are His mother and brothers. This was not natural, but something of resurrection. Even when He wept, He did not weep in a natural way. In His weeping there was also the fragrance of resurrection.

The fine flour signifies the humanity of Jesus, the oil signifies the divine Spirit, and the frankincense signifies the fragrance of resurrection life. This is the man Jesus: a life in humanity, mingled with the divine Spirit, and expressing something of resurrection life. This is the meal offering. Just a handful of this offering was burnt on the altar to God for His satisfaction as an eternal memorial, and the remainder, the greater part, was left for the priests. We all must learn to feed on Christ as this offering to be presented to God in the tent of meeting. We simply partake of the same Christ with God, and this will become our daily food. This food will transform us so that we have a priestly life, thus qualifying us to serve God as the priesthood.

CHAPTER FIVE

THE SPICES OF THE MEAL OFFERING

Scripture Reading: Lev. 2:4-16; 6:14-18

It is important to see the significance of the spices of the meal offering. There are always spices in a proper recipe. In the meal offering, there are three positive spices and two negative spices. The fine flour is not a spice, but is the main substance and ingredient for preparing the meal offering. Added to the fine flour are a number of spices mentioned in Leviticus 2.

THE OIL

The first spice is the oil. We have mentioned this in the previous chapter. We all know that in typology oil signifies the divine Spirit. I use the word "divine" instead of "holy" because Christians today have many deviant concepts related to the words "Holy Spirit." In this chapter I prefer to use divine Spirit, for the divine Spirit is just the divinity of God. The fine flour signifies the humanity of Jesus, and the oil signifies the divinity of Jesus. So the oil is the divine spice added to the meal offering.

Jesus is a man, yet He is mingled and anointed with the divine Spirit. The divine Spirit is not only mingled with the humanity of Jesus, but also anoints His humanity. The mingling is deeper than the anointing, but the anointing is more apparent. For instance, in Leviticus 2, the fine flour from the pan must be mingled with the oil. Then it becomes a certain form to be divided into portions. Then, after being divided into portions, oil is poured upon it. "And if thy oblation be a meal offering baked in a pan, it shall be of fine flour unleavened, mingled with oil. Thou shall part it in pieces, and pour oil thereon: it is a meal offering" (Lev. 2:5-6). After the mingling, there is still the need of the anointing. The mingling takes place within, inwardly, whereas the anointing is accomplished without, outwardly.

From His birth, Jesus was mingled with the Holy Spirit. He was born of the Holy Spirit; this means that His humanity was mingled already with the divine Spirit. But at the time He was baptized, the Holy Spirit descended upon Him in the form of a dove (Matt. 3:16). He was not only mingled within with the divine Spirit, but also anointed without with the divine Spirit in the form of a dove. He was not just anointed in an abstract way, but anointed with the Spirit in a definite form, as a dove. So we see that the oil, as a spice of the meal offering, was mingled with the fine flour and was also used to anoint the fine flour. Jesus, as our meal offering, was both mingled and anointed with the divine Spirit.

THE FRANKINCENSE

The second spice in the meal offering is frankincense. In typology, frankincense signifies the fragrance of the resurrection life and nature of Christ. Even before He was crucified and resurrected, there was always something so sweet and fragrant in all His behavior and activities. That was the resurrection life. In the humanity of Jesus, the meal offering, there is the spice of the divine Spirit and the spice of the resurrection life.

SALT

Another positive spice is salt. It is easy to understand the meaning of salt. Salt, first of all, kills the germs of corruption. And as it kills the corrupting elements, it also preserves, thus imparting lasting power. Salt has killing power, preserving power, and lasting power.

When we read the biography of Jesus in the four Gospels, we see that all His activities on the earth are forever. The ages have changed and the centuries have passed away, but the life of Jesus is still here. It really has lasting power. There is continually a kind of preserving in the life, activities, and behavior of the Lord Jesus. His activities are not like the activities of a natural man. Some of man's activities were good in the second century, but not today. Some were good just thirty years ago, but today no one would be interested. They are over. Read the four Gospels again. Every page is so fresh and new. Everything the Lord Jesus did is still so refreshing. Nothing could damage His activity, for there was no element of corruption within it. All the corrupting elements cannot exist with the heavenly salt in the life of Jesus. Hence the life of the Lord Jesus will last for eternity. I do believe that in the New Jerusalem we will often recall the pages of the four Gospels.

In the life of the Lord Jesus, especially in His humanity, there is the salt. This is the killing power, the preserving power, and the lasting power. His love to us is so pure. Many times the love we have toward others has almost no salt. It was sweet yesterday, but it has become bitter today. This is because there is no salt. Without salt, our love becomes fermented. We must put salt into all our relationships with the brothers. To like a certain brother is good, but this kind of relationship needs to be killed. I do not mean the liking of that brother needs to be killed, but the corrupting elements in the liking must be killed. There is the need of the killing power in the salt.

Hallelujah! the humanity of Jesus has the oil, the frankincense, and the salt. When Lazarus, the most intimate friend of Jesus, became sick, his sisters, Martha and Mary, sent the news to Jesus, telling Him that the one He loved was sick. If we had been Jesus, we probably would have shed a few tears and gone to see him immediately. But after Jesus received the report, it seems that He was not moved. He stayed where He was for several days. Do not think that He did not love Lazarus. He loved him, but within His love there was the killing power, the killing of anything corrupting. His love was a pure love; therefore, it was a lasting love.

If you tell me that a certain brother whom I know very well is sick, it will be a real test to me. If I become sorrowful and say that I must go immediately and see this brother, it proves that there is no salt, no killing power in my love. Surely this kind of love is easily stirred up. It is emotional and natural. If, however, I have been experiencing the humanity of Jesus with the salt, when the report comes concerning this brother, I will immediately turn to the Lord: "Lord, what is Your feeling? I do not want to go by my natural feeling—that must be crossed out. If You do not have any feeling about this brother's sickness, then I will forget about it." We really need the salt to kill the natural friendships, the natural love, and the natural affection. The salt is not only for killing, but also for preserving power and for lasting power.

THE NEGATIVE SPICES

The oil, the frankincense, and the salt are the positive spices in the meal offering, but there are also some negative spices. By negative spices, I mean that these spices are never to be added to the meal offering. "No meal offering, which ye shall bring unto the Lord, shall be made with leaven: for ye shall burn no leaven, nor any honey, in any offering of the Lord made by fire" (Lev. 2:11). Why should we never add leaven or honey to the meal offering? It is because these two things can be easily fermented. When fermentation begins in any food, that food is corrupted and damaged.

The first negative spice mentioned is leaven. Leaven in the Bible always signifies evil things. Worldliness, sinfulness, anything related to corruption, and all evil things are likened in the Bible as leaven.

What then is honey? In the Bible honey signifies something good. Our hatred is leaven, and our love is honey. Our pride is leaven, and our humility is honey. All our good behavior is honey. Our love may be good, but it can be fermented. In many cases, hatred does not ferment as much as love. Suppose five brothers are living together and hate one another. It would be rather difficult for them to be fermented, for they are so cold in their hatred. However, when they love one another too much, they are disarmed by their natural love. Within just a short time they may all become fermented.

In the church we do not need pride nor do we need humility. We do not like to have a brother who thinks he knows everything nor do we like to have a brother who always says he knows nothing. This is honey. Honey is so sweet and is so deceitful. We know that hatred is bad, but no one would say that love is bad. But Leviticus 2 says that we should not put any leaven or honey in the meal offering. No leaven or honey will be accepted by God. They will not ascend from the altar as a kind of sweet savor to the Lord.

We must neither be proud nor humble. We must simply take the oil and the frankincense with a certain amount of salt. This is the Spirit, the resurrection, and the cross. The salt is just the cross to cross out our natural love, our natural affection, and our natural patience. All these "good" things must be crossed out, for they will cause fermentation. I am always afraid of a patient person. If you are patient with me all the time, one day you will be the most critical person in the world to me. Do not appreciate any kind of natural patience. All the natural goodness must be crossed out by the salt.

The salt is the cross and the frankincense is the resurrection. In the meal offering, which is the humanity of Jesus, there is the killing of the cross, and there is also the resurrection. The salt kills, preserves, and imparts lasting power, and the frankincense is the fragrant resurrection life. The salt in this chapter is called the salt of the covenant of God. "And every oblation of thy meal offering shalt thou season with salt; neither shalt thou suffer the salt of the covenant of thy God to be lacking from thy meal offering: with all thine offerings thou shalt offer salt" (Lev. 2:13). In the covenant that God has made with us, the basic factor is the cross, the crucifixion of the Lord. This causes His covenant to last forever. It is by the cross that it is made an everlasting covenant. Thus, in the meal offering there is the humanity of Christ, the divinity of Christ, the cross to kill and preserve, and the resurrection fragrance to flavor His whole humanity.

This should not be a mere doctrine to us. If we are feeding upon the meal offering, we will eventually become what we eat. We live by what we eat, and gradually what we eat becomes what we are. The meal offering includes the humanity of Jesus, the divinity of Jesus, the cross of Jesus, and the resurrection of Jesus. There is the fine flour, the oil, the frankincense, and the salt. There is no ground for any leaven or honey in this meal offering. In the life of Jesus as a man there is no place for any kind of impurity or corruption. If we are feeding on such a Jesus, we will have the fine flour, the oil, the salt, and the frankincense, without any leaven or honey.

THE DIFFERENT APPRECIATIONS
OF THE MEAL OFFERING

Leviticus 2 also reveals the different appreciations of Christ as the meal offering. We have already seen this with the burnt offering. There was the bullock, the sheep or goat, and the turtledove or young pigeon. The meal offering also has three kinds or degrees of appreciation. "And if thou bring an oblation of a meal offering baked in the oven, it shall be unleavened cakes of fine flour mingled with oil, or unleavened wafers anointed with oil. And if thy oblation be a meal offering baked in a pan, it shall be of fine flour unleavened, mingled with oil. And if thy oblation be a meal offering baked in the frying pan, it shall be made of fine flour with oil" (Lev. 2:4-5, 7).

In the burnt offering, the degree of appreciation differs in size, but in the appreciation of Jesus as the meal offering, there are the different degrees of sufferings. The oven signifies one kind of suffering; the pan signifies another kind of suffering; and the frying pan signifies still another kind of suffering.

When we put something into the oven, the suffering is within. It is a hidden suffering, a deeper kind of suffering. In the four Gospels, some of the sufferings of the Lord Jesus are just like the sufferings in the oven. They are so hidden that only He knows; others do not. For instance, when He was in the Garden of Gethsemane, He was praying, but even His disciples who were with Him did not know the extent of His suffering. He was really in a kind of oven. This is the deepest appreciation of the suffering Jesus. His suffering was inward, without any sympathy from others. He was put into an oven. Whether we present Christ as one suffering in the oven or in the pan depends upon our apprehension and experience. Our appreciation comes out of our apprehension and experience of Jesus.

The cakes and wafers which were baked in the oven were more definite in form. Every cake and every wafer is in a certain form. Our experience and appreciation of Jesus in this deeper way have something more of a definite form. The Hebrew word "cakes" which is used here means perforated cakes or pierced cakes. This is a cake that is perforated and full of holes. As we read the four Gospels, we see that Jesus was perfect, but He was not whole. He was perfect, but He was perforated and pierced through. I am afraid that with many of us there is not even one hole. We are not perfect, yet we are so whole. To be perfect is right, but we should not keep ourself so whole. In the church life, the more holes we have the better. We should not keep ourselves so whole that we are not broken, perforated, and pierced through.

The life of Jesus in the Gospels was one of piercing after piercing. This is why it is easy for us to feed upon Him. It is so easy to eat the perforated and pierced cakes.

The Hebrew word "wafers" means cakes that are very, very thin. Probably they were hollow, because the root of this word means "empty." It is so thin and so hollow; therefore, it is easy for people to eat. Yet His inward suffering in this way has a definite form. This is the deepest appreciation of Jesus as the meal offering. Some who bring Christ to the tent of meeting as the meal offering must have this deepest appreciation of His suffering.

The second appreciation of the meal offering is the fine flour mingled with oil and baked in a pan. A pan is more open than the oven. This signifies the open sufferings which are easier for others to realize. There is some form, for it is divided into portions, yet it is not so much in form as the cakes and wafers in the oven.

The third appreciation is the fine flour mingled with oil and baked in a frying pan. The suffering is more shallow, and there is almost no definite form. This is the lowest appreciation of Jesus as the meal offering. When we were first saved, most of us had this kind of appreciation of Jesus. But as we feed upon the Lord's humanity and grow, we should have at least a little appreciation of Jesus as the cakes and wafers baked in the oven. Our appreciation and experience of the Lord's humanity must become deeper and deeper, higher and higher, and much more definite in form.

THE MEAL OFFERING OF THE FIRSTFRUITS

Besides these three appreciations, there is the appreciation of the meal offering of the firstfruits. "And if thou present a meal offering of thy firstfruits unto the Lord, thou shalt present for the meal offering of thy first-fruits green ears of corn roasted by the fire, even corn beaten out of fresh and full ears" (Lev. 2:14, lit.). The new green corn is shelled out of the fresh ears. This is an extraordinary appreciation of Christ. The regular appreciations of Christ are those in three degrees, but besides these, there are the extraordinary appreciations of the humanity of Jesus. Sometimes we have some new experiences of Christ as our meal offering. Sometimes in the meetings, the testimony of a certain brother gives the sense of something really green, something new and fresh. Yet it is the meal offering. Therefore, we need to have more and more experiences of Christ. If we do not have a harvest, how can we have the green and fresh ears? We must labor on the good land with the expectation that some day we will have a new harvest with many fresh ears. Then we can bring this to the tent of meeting as a kind of extraordinary meal offering.

THE WAY TO EAT THE MEAL OFFERING

Only for the Priests

Now it is important for us to see the way to eat the meal offering. First of all, the meal offering is not for the common people. It is the special diet of the priests. "And the remainder thereof shall Aaron and his sons eat: with unleavened bread shall it be eaten in the holy place; in the court of the tabernacle of the congregation they shall eat it. All the males among the children of Aaron shall eat of it. It shall be a statute for ever in your generations concerning the offerings of the Lord made by fire: every one that toucheth them shall be holy" (Lev. 6:16, 18).

The meal offering is the food of the priests. If we have no intention to function in the church life as a priest, we do not have the standing to eat this diet. A priest is one who serves and is active in the tent of meeting. It makes a big difference whether or not we function in the meetings. If we will function, we will enjoy much more. But if we will not function, we will lose the standing to enjoy the meal offering as a priest. To be a priest we must function in a full way to enjoy the special diet of the meal offering.

Only for the Males

Another point is that the meal offering is only for the males. "All the males among the children of Aaron shall eat of it." This does not mean that the sisters do not have a portion. All the sisters who are functioning in the tent of meeting are males. And all the brothers who do not function are females. To be a male in the Scriptures means to be a strong one. Christ is the male without blemish. To be a female means to be a weaker one (1 Pet. 3:7). Males are the strong ones, and females are the weaker ones. Whether or not you are a male in the eyes of God depends on whether you are strong or weak. If we are weak in the tent of meeting, we are females. If we are strong in functioning, we are males and are in the right position to feed on this diet.

Only in the Tent of Meeting

The meal offering must be eaten in the court of the tent of meeting. This is not food that you eat at home. Strictly speaking, we cannot enjoy Christ properly as the meal offering at home; we must be in the church meetings. This is not a diet for home, but a diet for the house of God. We must be ones serving and actively working in the presence of God in His dwelling place; then we have the right position to eat this diet. Many of us can testify that while we enjoy something of Christ at home, we never enjoy Him as much there as we do in the church meeting. The enjoyment of Christ in the meeting is higher, richer, and without comparison. The meal offering may be prepared at home, but it cannot be enjoyed at home. We must bring what we have prepared to the church meeting for our enjoyment. This is a diet for the court of the tent of meeting.

With No Leaven or Honey

When we come to eat the meal offering, we should not eat it with any leaven or honey. The meal offering itself has no leaven or honey in it, and we should not eat any of these negative spices with this offering. To enjoy Christ as the meal offering, we should have nothing to do with leaven or honey. We must reject anything that is naturally bad or good in order to enjoy Christ in such a high way. We have to be salted. The only spices that we must use are the oil and the frankincense and the salt—the divine Spirit, the resurrection life, and the crossing out of the cross.

Sanctifying Whoever It Touches

The last point in the eating of the meal offering is that whoever touches it is sanctified, separated. I can testify that this is really true. Many times after we have enjoyed Christ as the meal offering in the meetings, we are more separated from the world. We are more separated, more sanctified, because we have been feasting upon the meal offering. When we really enjoy the Lord Jesus as the meal offering, we will be fully separated from anything worldly. Because the meal offering is so holy, whoever touches it is separated from the world to be holy for the Lord. Once we taste the Lord Jesus in this way, there will be a big change in our daily walk. He is so holy that He sanctifies, separates, and causes us to be holy. If we claim to be eating Him as the meal offering, yet we remain the same, I really doubt that we are eating Him as the meal offering. The real meal offering, which is Christ's humanity, is holy. Whosoever touches it is separated, sanctified, and made holy.

CHAPTER SIX

THE HUMANITY OF JESUS IN LUKE

Scripture Reading: Lev. 2:4-7; Luke 2:40, 49, 51-52; 3:21-22;
4:1, 13-14, 18a, 22a, 28-30; 5:15-16; 6:11-12; 9:55; 10:21; 11:53-54;
19:41, 47; 22:28, 44, 51, 61; 24:19

DIFFERENT DEGREES OF THE MEAL OFFERING

Before we consider the humanity of Jesus in Luke, I
feel that we still need to consider the appreciation of the
meal offering in different degrees. We mentioned in the
last chapter the different appreciations of the Lord Jesus
as the burnt offering and the meal offering. In each of
these two offerings, there are three degrees. With the
burnt offering there is the bullock, the sheep or goat, and
the turtledove or pigeon. This does not mean that there
are only three kinds of appreciations of Jesus as the burnt
offering. It simply means that there are many different
degrees. Some are higher, some are lower, and some are
between.

When we come to the meal offering, there are also
three degrees of appreciation of the Lord Jesus. There is
something out of the oven, something out of the pan, and
something out of the frying pan. We all know what an
oven is. It is an enclosed container for cooking or baking.
It is entirely enclosed, unlike the pan, which is open at
the top. Yet the pan is deeper than the frying pan, which
is the most open and shallow. All of these different cooking
utensils signify differing degrees of suffering. The suffering in the oven is the greatest. It is the deepest and most
hidden. It seems that nothing is going on, but something
is suffered in a hidden way.

In the pan, the suffering is not so hidden or deep. It is rather open to everybody. And the frying pan is even more shallow. Thus, we can see the suffering in these three kinds of cooking utensils. But we must realize that there is no difference with the Lord Jesus Himself; the difference is only in our appreciation, in our apprehension and understanding. How much we appreciate the Lord's suffering depends on how much we apprehend it. The appreciation comes out of our apprehension.

The cakes and the wafers in the oven are the most definite in form. Paul mentions in Galatians 4:19 that Christ must be formed in us. The cakes and wafers have a definite form. In the pan the fine flour is soaked and mingled with oil and divided into four portions. It is inferior in form to the cakes and wafers in the oven, but it is not inferior in substance. The substance is the same as the cakes and wafers, but the form is not as definite or full. In the frying pan, the third category, there is just some fine flour and a little bit of oil. It has almost no form. Nor does it say that the flour is mingled with the oil, but just that the fine flour is with the oil.

These three degrees should not be a mere doctrine to us. We must put these things into practice. I do believe that we have brought something of Christ as the meal offering to the tent of meeting. But there is the matter of degree. Is what we bring to the meeting definite in form and with the greatest suffering? Or is it just a little of Christ, not having such a definite form, and with only fine flour and a little oil from the frying pan. When I was young in the Lord, I appreciated Him so much. But now when I look back, I realize that my appreciation of the Lord at that time was just the meal offering baked in the frying pan. There was no form and not much suffering. By the Lord's mercy, I do believe that today I have some appreciation of the Lord as the cakes and wafers in the oven. It is definite in form and with a greater suffering.

THE PROPER WORSHIP IN REALITY

Whenever we come to the church meetings, we must come with something of Christ as the meal offering, and some of the more mature ones must come with a meal offering baked in the oven. Some of the younger ones will bring something of Christ as the meal offering from the frying pan. It is still good. We all must bring something of Christ to the meetings as the meal offering. We will present this as a kind of present to God to constitute the proper worship to Him in the meetings.

Strictly speaking, among today's Christians, there is the service, the work, the preaching, and the teaching, but there is almost no worship. The worship that God desires is that the people of God would bring the very Christ whom they have experienced in their daily life. Exodus, Leviticus, Numbers, and Deuteronomy were all written about the worship to God, but there is hardly a word telling us to bow down and prostrate ourselves before the Lord.

The Unique Place of Unity

These books tell us to worship God by first coming to the unique place of unity (Deut. 12:5-8, 14-15). There is no choice. All the people of Israel were destined to worship God by going to Jerusalem. Jerusalem was the unique place chosen by God. God's choice must be our destiny; we have no choice. As long as we are in Los Angeles, we have to worship God in the church in Los Angeles. Wherever we go, we must worship God in the church at that place. The local church and the proper ground of unity are our destiny. If we could have a choice in the place of worship, that would not be real worship. Real worship is on the ground of unique, genuine unity. All the people of Israel had to go to that one unique place chosen by God.

Hands Full of Produce

The second point concerning worship in these four

books is that everyone must come to Jerusalem with their hands full of the produce of the good land (Deut. 16:16-17). No one was to come with his hands empty. Each had to have something to offer to God, and that offering was the real worship to God. Today, in principle, it is exactly the same. Whenever we come together in the church meetings, the important matter is how much of Christ we bring. In the proper worship meeting, all the saints must bring something of Christ—not Christ in teaching or in doctrine, but Christ in their experiences.

The people of Israel first of all had to labor on the good land. They had to till the land, sow the seed, and reap the harvest. Afterward they had to grind the grains to obtain the flour for the meal offering. Then when they came together to worship God, they had something to bring and present to God as real worship. Today the Lord is going to recover this worship not only in spirit, but also in reality. Reality is just Christ as so many kinds of offerings.

If we come to the Lord with our hands empty and bow down and say, "O Lord, we have come to worship You," the Lord will say that He does not desire this kind of worship. He prefers that we stay home and work on Christ and then come with something of Christ in our hand. Only Christ constitutes real worship to God. Anything else is just a kind of religion, not worship. God is mainly concerned with how much Christ we bring to the meetings.

When the Samaritan woman spoke with the Lord, she told Him how the Jews insisted to worship in Jerusalem, but her fathers worshipped God in another place. The Lord Jesus then told her that the dispensation had been changed. Real worship to God is not in this place, but in spirit and in reality (John 4:20-24). The reality is Christ as all the offerings typified in the Old Testament. We must have something of Christ experienced by us to bring to the tent of meeting, which are the meetings of the local church.

FOUR ITEMS OF THE LORD'S HUMANITY IN LUKE

Now we come to the humanity of Christ as seen in the Gospel of Luke. If we would experience Christ's humanity, we need to pray-read all these verses in Luke that we have listed. None of them are in any of the other Gospels. These verses are unique to the Gospel of Luke because this Gospel more than any other reveals the humanity of Christ.

The Fine Flour

All these verses in Luke cover four main points. First of all they show Jesus as the fine flour. He is so fine and balanced. Luke 2:40 says, "And the child grew, and waxed strong in spirit, filled with wisdom: and the grace of God was upon him." He was growing, but He was also strong in spirit. Sometimes the young ones grow physically, but they are not strong in spirit. With Jesus there was not only the growth in His physical life, but also the strengthening in His spirit. He was so balanced, even with the four things in this one verse. He grew and waxed strong in spirit. He was full of wisdom, and the grace of God was upon Him. He had growth, a strong spirit, wisdom, and the grace of God. He was really balanced, not only in two or three ways, but in four ways.

The same chapter in Luke tells us that when He was twelve years of age, He knew how to care for His Father's will and yet at the same time be subject to His natural parents. He both rebuked His parents and was subject unto them. He asked, "Wist ye not that I must be about my Father's business?" (Luke 2:49). Yet verse 51 says that He went with them and was subject unto them. Do you see the balance? Some young people may say, "I am for God; I do not care for my parents." Yes, they are for God, but they are not balanced. When they are still under age, as Jesus was when He was twelve, they must be for God, yet at the same time be subject to their parents. So many young people are for Jesus, but in a rough way. They are not fine and balanced.

62 CHRIST AS THE REALITY

Luke 2:52 says that Jesus as a child found favor with
both God and man. To find favor with God is one thing,
but to find favor with man is another. Jesus was so
balanced, so fine, and so even, but we are so unbalanced.
We may be good, but in an unbalanced way; thus we are
not the fine flour, but the coarse flour. When the Lord
Jesus was young, He was wholly for His heavenly Father,
yet He was willing to be balanced. We really see Jesus as the fine flour in the Gospel of
Luke. He rejoiced, but He also wept. I am afraid that
many of us have never wept, and some in the past years
have never rejoiced. We are not so balanced. Some are too
quiet and need to make a little noise, and some noisy ones
need to be quieter. We all must be balanced. Luke 10:21
says that Jesus rejoiced in spirit, but it was not for
Himself; He rejoiced in the will of God. "In that hour
Jesus rejoiced in spirit, and said, I thank thee, O Father,
Lord of heaven and earth, that thou hast hid these things
from the wise and prudent, and hast revealed them unto
babes: even so, Father; for so it seemed good in thy sight."
He rejoiced because the Father had revealed all these
things to the babes. Luke 19:41 says that He wept over
Jerusalem: "And when he was come near, he beheld the
city, and wept over it." He was not weeping for Himself,
but for the situation of the city of Jerusalem.

We all must be balanced. When we need to rejoice, we
must rejoice. When we need to weep, we must weep. Jesus,
the balanced man, lives today in us! The very Jesus who
is our life is the rejoicing One as well as the weeping One.
If we have never rejoiced, if we have never wept, it simply
proves that we are not experiencing the man Jesus as our
life. If we do take Him as our life, when He weeps, we
will weep; when He rejoices, we will rejoice.

How we need to pray-read all these verses in Luke
that we may really see Jesus as the fine flour! When He
sent His disciples to a place in Samaria, the people
rejected them. So the disciples said, "Lord, wilt thou that
we command fire to come down from heaven, and consume

them, even as Elias did?" But He turned and rebuked them and said, "Ye know not what manner of spirit ye are of" (Luke 9:54-55). He was so fine. Whether the people rejected Him or welcomed Him, He was continually the same. No rejection could irritate or offend Him. When people welcomed Him, He went away. "But so much the more went there a fame abroad of him: and great multitudes came together to hear, and to be healed by him of their infirmities. And he withdrew himself into the wilderness, and prayed" (Luke 5:15-16). We would think that when His fame grew it would be a great opportunity for Him to do something. But He withdrew Himself and went into the wilderness to pray. When people welcomed Him, He went away, and when people rejected Him, He was patient with them. All these verses reveal to us a man who is really the fine flour. He is so tender, so kind, so even, so balanced, so gentle, and so pure.

The Oil

Second, we can see in these verses something of the oil. He was born of the Spirit, and the Spirit even descended upon Him in the bodily form of a dove. "Now when all the people were baptized, it came to pass, that Jesus also being baptized, and praying, the heaven was opened, and the Holy Spirit (lit.) descended in a bodily shape like a dove upon him, and a voice came from heaven, which said, Thou art my beloved Son; in thee I am well pleased" (Luke 3:21-22). The Spirit did not descend upon Him in an abstract way, but in a definite form. He was full of the Spirit, led by the Spirit, and in the power of the Spirit: "And Jesus being full of the Holy Spirit (lit.) returned from Jordan, and was led by the Spirit into the wilderness....And Jesus returned in the power of the Spirit into Galilee" (Luke 4:1, 14). He was even anointed with the Spirit: "The Spirit of the Lord is upon me, because he hath anointed me..." (Luke 4:18). With the humanity of Jesus as the fine flour, there is the oil as the Spirit anointing, mingling, and saturating Him.

The Frankincense

We can also see something of the fragrant frankincense in these verses. He was so fragrant and so sweet. It is very difficult to translate this word "frankincense." Some versions say that this is something restful and satisfying. It is not only sweet and fragrant, but restful and peaceful. In all these verses we see that Jesus is really the fragrant frankincense. He has the fragrance of the resurrection. When Jesus was being arrested, Peter was strong with his sword to cut off the ear of one of the servants. But the Lord Jesus told Peter, "Suffer ye thus far. And he touched his ear, and healed him" (Luke 22:51). Jesus stopped the sword and recovered the ear. This is not anything natural; this is the fragrance of His resurrection. In His most tested hour, Jesus would not accept any protection; He cared instead for the suffering one.

The Salt

In these verses we can see the fine flour, the oil, the frankincense, and also the salt. When people wanted to make Him great, He ran away. When they rejected Him, He did not reprove them. When they arrested Him, He could have destroyed them by calling twelve legions of angels, but He did nothing (Matt. 26:53). He even healed the ear of the one who came to arrest Him. What is this? This is the killing of the self. There was no corruption or fermentation with Him. He was under the salt all of the time. Regardless of what kind of situation or circumstance He was in, He was always under the killing in His actions and words. In His human living, there was the real salt. So in Jesus, we see the fine flour, the oil, the frankincense, and the salt.

The Gospel of Luke is strategic in showing us the Lord's humanity. This is why we cannot find these verses in the other three Gospels. These are the unique verses concerning the humanity of Jesus. We all need to pray-read these verses at least three or four times, and put them into practice in our daily walk. It is only by feeding upon His humanity in these verses that we will experience His humanity in our daily life.

REAL WORSHIP

What the Lord is seeking today is the local churches where the saints worship God with their experiences of Christ. This is the real offering to God. We need to experience Christ in our daily walk, and we must learn how to cook and prepare Christ that we may bring Him to the meetings for a present to God. All the cakes, wafers, and portions of the meal offering were made and cooked at home and then brought to the tent of meeting. It is the same with us. Day by day we need to work on Christ: experience Him, enjoy Him, apprehend Him, and cook Him a little. We will then have something to bring to the meeting and present to God. This is the real worship, and this is the real recovery of the church life in all the localities. It is not just a matter of meeting together, but of meeting with Christ as all kinds of offerings. It is by this that we are united, and it is also by this that we render our worship to God. It is absolutely different from today's so-called Christian service. May the Lord be merciful to us that we may be faithful to Him in this matter.

Chapter Seven

THE HUMANITY OF JESUS
IN MATTHEW, MARK, AND JOHN

Scripture Reading: Matt. 3:15; 4:4, 7, 10; 8:20; 11:29; 12:19-20;
17:27; 20:28; 21:27; 26:63-64; 27:12, 14; Mark 1:35; 3:20-21;
6:31, 39-40; John 6:12; 7:6, 46; 11:33, 35, 38; 13:4-5

The four Gospels give us a full picture of the Lord
Jesus from four directions. I believe we all know that
Matthew reveals the Lord Jesus as the King. Mark shows
us a picture of Him as the slave, the servant of God. Luke
portrays the Lord Jesus as the perfect man. The last
Gospel, John, reveals that Christ is God Himself; He is
the Son of God. So from these four Gospels we obtain four
words: King, Servant, Man, and God. The Lord Jesus is
so much! He is the King; He is the Servant; He is the
Man; and He is also the very God. But what He is in all
these directions and aspects depends upon His humanity.
That is why in all the Gospels there are verses concerning
His humanity.

WOOD OVERLAID
WITH GOLD

Let me illustrate in this way. Among the types in the
Old Testament, there is the ark made of wood overlaid
with gold. The wood, not the gold, is the frame of the ark.
The gold gives the beauty, the worth, and the value,
but the gold is not the frame. The gold is the decoration
upon the wood. The frame and the main basic structure
that holds and supports the gold is the wood. In typology,
wood signifies humanity; hence, this wood of the ark

signifies the humanity of Christ. The humanity of Christ is the basic structure that supports the gold of the ark.

The tabernacle is built with forty-eight wooden boards which are the frame of the tabernacle. This means that the humanity of Jesus is the frame of the tabernacle. If He were not a proper man, He could never be the King, the Servant, and the perfect Man. The very God revealed in John is not God alone, but a God-man; He is God in man. But if Jesus were not a perfect man, how could God be incarnated in Him? If Jesus were not perfect and God was incarnated in Him, God would be depreciated and lose His value. The divine value, however, is complemented by a perfect humanity. It was a complete, solid, and perfect humanity in which God could be contained in a full way. Even for Jesus to be God requires the humanity of Jesus. If He were not a perfect man, He could never be the King, the Servant, the Man, or the very God incarnated in a man. All these aspects of the Lord Jesus depend upon His humanity.

How we need such a humanity today in the church life! We have already seen that the ark is the type of Christ, and the tabernacle is the type of the church. The tabernacle is the enlargement of the ark. In the same way today the church is the enlargement of Christ. If it is necessary for Christ to have such a humanity to be God's testimony, then we as the church also need the same strong and perfect humanity.

THE BASIC STRUCTURE

Wood is the basic structure of the ark, and wood is also the main structure of the tabernacle. Hence, it is the humanity of Jesus that is the main structure of Christ as God's testimony, and it is the humanity of Jesus that is the basic structure of the church life. If we do not have this humanity, as typified by acacia wood, it is impossible for us to have a proper church as the Body of Christ. For a real building up of the Body of Christ in our locality, we all need the humanity of Jesus. There is only one kind of wood that is good for the structure of both the ark and the tabernacle—that is acacia wood. And there is only one kind of humanity that is good for God's testimony today in the local church life—that is the humanity of Jesus.

Our humanity is not good for God's building. Many of us may be good, but regardless of how good we are, our humanity is of no use. It may be useful for many other things, but not for the church life. For the building up of the ark and the tabernacle, there is only one kind of wood which is useful—that is the acacia wood, the humanity of Jesus.

Many people today say that all we need is the baptism of the Holy Spirit, the outpouring from above. That is wonderful, but consider yourself: what kind of humanity do you have? The Spirit is typified by the gold, but this is not the basic structure. The basic structure is the wood. Suppose we were going to build a tabernacle and had tons of gold, yet the wood we used was rotten. That tabernacle would not stand. Regardless of how much gold we have, without the proper wood, we can never build a tabernacle. I have seen people praying, seeking, and crying for the baptism of the Holy Spirit, and eventually they received it. But their building fell apart. It was not due to the gold, but to the poor quality of the wood. This is the thing that is neglected by today's Christianity. Today's Christians pay much attention to the baptism of the Holy Spirit, but where is the proper humanity? The tabernacle as a type of the church was not built purely with the gold. It was built with the wood as the main structure. The gold was just a kind of decoration. Of course, without the overlaying gold, there would be little value or beauty. The wood alone is not of much worth. But although the value is in the gold, gold is not the main structure. The gold requires something solid to support it. That is the proper, solid, strong, and perfect humanity. Do we have such a humanity? We do not have it in ourselves, but we do have it in Christ. He is the perfect humanity within us.

THE HUMANITY OF JESUS
IN MATTHEW

If we would pray-read all the verses in Matthew concerning the Lord's humanity, we would see the humanity it takes to be a king. Many years ago, a Christian teacher argued with me, saying that we would all be kings when the Lord comes back. But I asked, "Brother, look at yourself. Could you be a king?" Do you believe that we can be so sloppy in our humanity now, yet when the Lord Jesus returns He will suddenly make us a king? Such teachings are nonsense.

No Exception

All that the Lord is in His person depends upon His humanity. Look at the verses in Matthew. John the Baptist was baptizing in the Jordan. Even John saw that there was no need for Jesus to be baptized. He was the Son of God. Nevertheless, Jesus said, "Permit it now, for in this way it is fitting for us to fulfill all righteousness" (Matt. 3:15). We must be so right with God in whatever He wants. Sometimes we, and especially the younger brothers and sisters, think that it may be necessary for others to do certain things, but not us. However, Jesus in effect said to John, "Regardless of who I am, as long as I am a man in this age, I must be baptized by you. This is what God is doing today. As long as I am living in this day of God's dispensation, I must go along with God's righteousness." This is the humanity of Jesus. We should never consider ourselves an exception. We need to fulfill all the righteousness of God.

Kept in the
Position of Man

After His baptism the man Jesus was led into the wilderness to be tempted by the evil one. Satan is so subtle. He said, "If You are the Son of God..." But the Lord immediately answered, "Man shall not live on bread alone..." (Matt. 4:3-4). In effect the Lord said to Satan,

"Do not put me in the position of the Son of God. I am here as a man. If I am here as the Son of God, how could I be tempted by you? I can be tempted only because I am a man. Undoubtedly I am the Son of God, but I am not standing in that position; I am standing here as a man."

Then the subtle one brought Him to the top of the temple and said, "If You are the Son of God, cast Yourself down; for it is written, He shall give charge to His angels concerning You, and on their hands they shall bear You up, lest You strike Your foot against a stone. Jesus said to him, Again it is written, You shall not tempt the Lord your God" (Matt. 4:6-7). Jesus told him that as a man He would never tempt God. Finally, Satan even attempted to persuade the Lord to worship him by offering Him the kingdoms of the world. But Jesus answered, "Go, Satan! For it is written, You shall worship the Lord your God, and Him only shall you serve" (Matt. 4:10). The Lord kept Himself continually in the position of man.

There is one more interesting matter in these verses concerning the temptation in the wilderness. Satan tempted the Lord Jesus by quoting Psalm 91. Even Satan can quote the Bible. But the Lord answered, "Again it is written." It is not a matter of quoting one passage of Scripture. There must be another for confirmation. This is the humanity of Jesus, quoting Scripture not in an isolated way, but in the way of confirmation.

No Resting Place

Matthew 8:20 says, "The foxes have holes, and the birds of the heaven have roosts, but the Son of Man has nowhere that He may lay His head." As a man, the Lord was not so comfortable all the time. Let us apply it in this way. Suppose five brothers move into an apartment with three bedrooms. Who will take the one bedroom for himself? If we seek a way to get the single bedroom for ourselves, that means that we are taking the humanity of foxes, not the humanity of Jesus. If we really take the Lord as our humanity, we will have no desire for the single bedroom. So many times we simply follow the foxes and birds of the air. The humanity that likes to have the fox's hole is of no use for the church life. Only the life that is willing to have nowhere to lay its head is good for the church. This is the humanity of Jesus, and this is the proper way to build up God's dwelling place. We all need such a humanity.

Lowly in Heart

Later on in Matthew the Lord Jesus says, "Take My yoke on you and learn from Me; for I am meek and lowly in heart" (Matt. 11:29). Jesus did not say that He was meek and lowly in appearance, but in heart. Many times we may appear so meek and lowly, but within we are high and proud. This can never build up the church life. Our own humanity can only give an appearance, but we do have His humanity within us that is meek and lowly in heart. We should not imitate Him; if we do, we will fail. We must simply feed upon Him as the meal offering. Isn't this wonderful! This perfect humanity can be our food. Then we will live by what we eat. His humanity will become our person.

Love for
the Weak Ones

In Matthew 12:19-20, there is a quotation from Isaiah: "He shall not strive nor cry out, nor shall anyone hear His voice in the streets. A bruised reed He shall not break, and smoking flax He shall not quench until He brings forth judgment unto victory." I really like these two verses. The Lord's humanity is so fine, never striving or crying out or making His voice famous in the streets. Many times we like for people to hear our voice. But this is not the Lord's humanity. Moreover, He would never break a bruised reed, nor would He quench smoking flax. To understand this, we must see something of the background of the Jewish people.

In the days of the Old Testament, the Jewish children

made music pipes out of reeds. But when the reed was bruised, it would not produce proper music, so they would break it. Some of us may be bruised reeds which do not produce proper music. But hallelujah, the Lord Jesus will never break such a bruised reed!

The Jews in the Old Testament days also used flax soaked with oil for a torch to give light at night. When the torch ran out of oil, it did not give light any more; it only smoked. Then the user would quench it and throw it away. But Jesus would never do this. Many times some believers are "smoking" because they have run out of oil. Our tendency is to throw them away, but the humanity of Jesus would not. How we need such a humanity in the church life!

We all love the pipe that makes beautiful music. But if someone is a bruised reed that makes a bad sound, we just say, "Break it." We like one brother because he is so bright and shining, but we do not like another because he is so smoky. This is why many times we are not able to hold the younger and weaker ones. We really need the humanity of Jesus not to break the bruised reeds and not to quench the smoking flax. The Lord's humanity loves all the bruised and smoking ones. We must have His humanity in the church life. By eating Jesus we can partake of His humanity.

Flexible

We are all familiar with the story in Matthew 17. Since Jesus was the Son of God, He was free from the tribute paid to God's temple. He made this clear to Peter. Then Jesus said, "But that we may not stumble them, go to the sea and cast an hook, and take the first fish that comes up, and when you open its mouth you will find a shekel; take that and give it to them for Me and you" (Matt. 17:27). Jesus was very flexible. He did not have to pay the tribute money, but lest He should offend, He paid it. He made the situation clear to His disciples, but He did not insist. He was clear, yet He exercised Himself in such a flexible way. This is His humanity.

Our humanity is completely different from this. Both the older and the younger ones always insist on their own way. Only the humanity of Jesus can be so flexible. I was in a place recently where both the older saints and the younger saints came to me. The older ones said that they could not tolerate the young people because they were too bold, too loud, and too wild. Perhaps the young people were indeed inclined that way. But do you know what I told the older ones? I said, "You may be right, and they may be wrong, but the Lord Jesus still loves them. Don't you think that it is much better for them to praise the Lord in this way than to go to the movies?" They had to agree that this was right from that point of view. I encouraged them to be a little flexible and to say some "hallelujahs" with the crazy young people.

Then I turned to the young people. They had told me that the older ones were so dead; therefore, I told them that they needed the older ones for a balance. Without the older ones they would be like a car without brakes. So they agreed to be also a little flexible and to accept the balance from the older ones. Not long ago I received a report from that place. The church life there is now so wonderful. We were told that there is wonderful coordination among the older ones and the younger ones. Both groups had learned to be flexible.

This is the humanity of Jesus. As the Son of God He was absolutely right in not paying anything to the temple, yet He paid. Furthermore, He not only paid for Himself, but also for Peter in order not to offend the people. In the church life, we must learn never to insist on anything, but to be flexible. Then we will not offend others. This is the humanity of Jesus.

A Serving Humanity

In Matthew 20:28 the Lord said, "The Son of Man came not to be served, but to serve." So many, especially

some of the young people who are living together, want
to be served, but they never serve. They do not clean the
house; they do not wash the dishes; they do not take care
of their clothing; they do not do anything. They just like
to sleep, rest, and enjoy life among the brothers and
sisters. This is not the humanity for the church life. The
humanity of the church life is one to serve, not to
be served. We even have to serve at the cost of our life.
We do need such a spirit to serve others. This can come
only from the humanity of Jesus.

A Real Man

When the Lord Jesus came to Jerusalem for the last
time, the chief priests and the elders asked Him where
He got the authority to do the things that He was doing.
The Lord Jesus was a proper man; He did not answer
them. Sometimes it is better not to answer, but to turn
the question to the one who asks. This is what Jesus did.
He asked them whether the baptism of John was from
heaven or of man. If they answered Him, He would tell
them where He got His authority. So they reasoned
together and realized that if they were to say that John's
baptism was from heaven, He would ask why they had
not believed him. And if they were to say that John's
baptism was from man, the people would stone them because all believed that John was a prophet. So their best
answer was to tell a lie. Therefore, they answered, "We
do not know. He also said to them, Neither do I tell you
by what authority I do these things" (Matt. 21:27). By
this the Lord indicated that it was not that they did not
know, but that they did not want to tell Him. They lied,
but He would not lie. Because they would not tell Him,
neither would He tell them. He had such a humanity.

When He was being judged before His crucifixion, the
high priest asked whether or not He was the Son of God.
The Lord Jesus replied, "You said it! Moreover, I say
to you, Henceforth you shall see the Son of Man sitting
at the right hand of power and coming on the clouds of

heaven" (Matt. 26:64). At the beginning of the book of Matthew the Lord took His standing as a man, and at the end of the book He still stood as a man. He said that the Son of Man would sit in the heavens at the right hand of God, and the Son of Man would come on the clouds of heaven. He will be the Son of Man forever. He will never leave this standing.

Later, when He was accused by the chief priests and elders, He answered nothing. They all marveled greatly at Him. "And when He was accused by the chief priests and elders, He answered nothing....And He did not answer him, not even to one word, so that the governor marveled greatly" (Matt. 27:12, 14). Many times if we would be quiet, others would marvel at us. We make ourselves cheap by talking too much. The more we talk, the more we cheapen ourselves. The Man portrayed in the Gospel of Matthew did not say anything when it was not necessary. What a humanity we see in this book!

THE HUMANITY OF JESUS
IN MARK

Diligent

Now we must go on to the Gospel of Mark. Mark tells us clearly that Christ is the servant of God. But what kind of man is this servant? First of all, He is a very diligent man. Mark 1 reveals that He was exceedingly busy. I do believe that He went to bed quite late; yet verse 35 says, "And in the morning, rising up a great while before day, he went out, and departed into a solitary place, and there prayed." Many times people excuse themselves for not rising early because they have gone to bed so late. They feel that they can make it only to the "eleven o'clock worship service." But the humanity which is only good for the so-called eleven o'clock service can never be good for the church life. It is only good for the eleven o'clock service. The church life needs a humanity that is diligent and alert. Sometimes the Lord was so busy that He did not have time even to eat. His relatives said that He was beside Himself (Mark 3:20-21), but sometimes we need to be the kind of man that is beside himself. The people who would not be beside themselves are usually those who are lazy. If a person is diligent in the things of the Lord, others may say that he is beside himself.

The same thing occurred in Mark 6. The Lord and His disciples were very busy, and many were coming and going so that they had no time to eat. "Come ye yourselves apart into a desert place, and rest a while" (Mark 6:31). Though sometimes He was beside Himself, yet at other times He withdrew from everyone. He did this not only to rest in body, but also in spirit. He was so balanced. Sometimes we must be busy, and at other times we need to stay away to rest our body and our spirit. This is the real balanced humanity.

Orderly

Later on in Mark 6, we see something more of the Lord's humanity. When He was feeding the five thousand, He commanded the disciples to make all the people sit down by companies. This was His wisdom. If they had not sat down, the disciples would not have been able to distribute the bread to them. The Lord Jesus did not tell them to sit down in a loose way, but in a very orderly way: "And he commanded them to make all sit down by companies upon the green grass. And they sat down in ranks, by hundreds, and by fifties" (Mark 6:39-40). Everything was arranged in order. I do believe that Peter and the other disciples learned in this way how to handle a large number of people. Therefore, it was not difficult to handle the three thousand who were saved at Pentecost (Acts 2:41). They learned from the Lord how to manage such a multitude and how to do things with proper arrangement. To have such an arrangement requires the proper humanity.

THE HUMANITY OF JESUS
IN JOHN

Not Sloppy

The Gospel of John also records something of the Lord's humanity. This Gospel adds something concerning the feeding of the five thousand. Jesus told the disciples to gather the pieces left over that nothing be lost (John 6:12). Here we see a humanity that is so solid. There is nothing sloppy in His behavior. Most of us would forget about all the fragments, but the Lord was careful not to leave anything in a sloppy way.

Limited by Time

In John 7:6, we see that the Lord was always limited by time. "Then Jesus said to them, My time has not yet come, but your time is always ready." All of us, especially the young people, need to learn not to be so free. Too much freedom indicates lawlessness. Freedom must be within the limits of law. We should not say that our time is always ready. The humanity of Jesus is not always so. His humanity does not have so much freedom. If we learn to partake of His humanity, we will see that there is limitation.

Unique

Something more about the humanity of Jesus is seen in John 7:46. The chief priests and Pharisees sent certain deputies to capture the Lord, but when they returned they said, "No man ever spoke as this man speaks." They had never seen a man like Jesus. We need to be such a man that others would say they have never seen anyone like us. We should be unique, because we enjoy such a unique humanity.

Knowing When to Weep

When Lazarus died, we read that Jesus groaned in His spirit and wept (John 11:33, 35). Many times I have thought that Jesus could never weep. But with His humanity, there is a time to weep. We should not be so strong that we never weep. I am afraid that if I were to weep in front of you, you would think that I am not strong. This is a religious concept; sometimes we need to weep. This is the real humanity.

Humble

Jesus not only served, but was also willing to wash the feet of His disciples. He "rose from supper and laid aside His garments; and taking a towel, He girded Himself. Then He poured water into the basin and began to wash the disciples' feet and to wipe them with the towel with which He was girded" (John 13:4-5). He had such a humanity. He was willing to wash their feet, instead of expecting them to wash His. How we need this humanity for the church life! It is so clear in these Gospels that Jesus' humanity was the highest humanity. This is the real meal offering.

FOOD FOR PRIESTS

We must realize again that the major part of the meal offering was food for the priests. If we are going to have the priest's life, we must take Jesus as our meal offering. There is a real shortage of the priesthood today because there is no food for the priests. Without proper food for the priest, there can be no priesthood. This cannot be just a doctrine among us. We need the life of the priesthood, and the life of the priesthood can be sustained only by this kind of food. This is not an ordinary diet, but a special, extraordinary diet that requires much labor on Christ. We must prepare something of Christ and bring it to the tent of meeting to present to God as a kind of memorial. The remainder will then be our food, and this food will sustain the life of the priesthood.

CHAPTER EIGHT

THE BOUNDLESS SUPPLY
OF THE HUMANITY OF JESUS

Scripture Reading: Gen. 3:15; 22:18a; Gal. 3:16; Rom. 5:15b, 19;
1 Cor. 15:21; 1 Tim. 2:5; Heb. 2:9, 14-18; Rev. 1:13; John 19:5

TWO EXTREMES

In Christianity, there are two extreme views concerning
the Person of Jesus. The modernists talk much about Jesus
as a man. They say that Jesus was only a Jewish man,
denying the Lord's divinity and not recognizing that He is
the very God incarnated to be a man. In other words, they
do not recognize the incarnation. Of course, this is not
just an extreme teaching, but the greatest heresy on the
earth and in the universe. Not to recognize that Jesus was
God incarnated to be a man is the greatest heresy.

Due possibly to the heresy of the modernists, the
fundamental Christians have gone to another extreme.
They preach and teach so much concerning Christ as the
Son of God. There is nothing wrong with this, but they
have neglected the humanity of Jesus. They stress the
divinity of Christ so much, but they teach and preach
very little regarding the humanity of Christ. This is the
hidden subtlety of the enemy. On the one hand the enemy
would not let people believe that the Lord Jesus is the
Son of God, and on the other hand the subtle one would
have us preach concerning His divinity while neglecting
the Lord's humanity. We must realize that although Christ
is the Son of God, whatever He did, and all that He is
today depends not only on His divinity, but even more on
His humanity.

We have mentioned that the basic framework and structure of the ark and the tabernacle was not gold, but wood. This signifies that what Christ is and what He has done does not depend on the divine nature so much as on the human nature. The humanity of Christ is the main structure. He is God, but whatever He did and whatever He is today requires His humanity.

A DIFFERENT SOURCE

We must be clear, however, that His humanity is not of the same source as ours. This is why we were born of men and He was born of a woman. We are the descendants of man, but He was the seed of a woman. Both He and we are human, but the sources are different. He is a man, but He is a man of a different category. Yet it is meaningful and wonderful that these two sources are very much related to one another. Only the Holy Spirit can make this matter clear to us. The woman was also a descendant of our source, but Jesus did not come from that source. Jesus came from the woman, from another source. This other source has something to do with our source, yet the two are different.

He took humanity upon Himself, and this very humanity is the main structure for Him to destroy the serpent, the enemy of God. It is by this structure, this humanity, that God could bring the blessing upon all the nations of the earth. "And I will put enmity between thee and the woman, and between thy seed and her seed; He shall bruise thy head, and thou shalt bruise his heel" (Gen. 3:15). "And in thy [Abraham's] seed shall all the nations of the earth be blessed" (Gen. 22:18a). "But to Abraham were the promises spoken and to his seed. He does not say, And to the seeds, as concerning many, but as concerning one, And to your seed, Who is Christ" (Gal. 3:16). Satan, the serpent, was bruised and destroyed by this humanity, and the blessing of God came to all the nations on the earth through this humanity. Even the grace with all its gifts abounded by this humanity. "For if through the offense of the one the many died, much

more the grace of God and the gift in grace of the One
Man Jesus Christ have abounded to the many" (Rom.
5:15b).

CONSTITUTED RIGHTEOUS

We were also constituted righteous by this man. "For
as through the disobedience of one man the many were
constituted sinners, so through the obedience of the One
shall the many be constituted righteous" (Rom. 5:19).
By the one man, Adam, we were all constituted sinners,
but by another man, Jesus, we were all constituted
righteous. We were made righteous simply by this man
alone.

We appreciate the work and the teachings of Martin
Luther. He pioneered God's recovery by recovering the
teaching of justification by faith. He fought the battle
against the Catholic Church on this matter, saying that
if man is to be justified by God, it is not by works, but
by faith. While this is right, I feel today we must tell
people that justification is just Christ. Today some
Lutheran pastors hold the teaching of justification by
faith, yet they themselves have never been justified. They
hold the doctrine, but they are not in Christ. There may
be a person who knows nothing concerning justification
by faith, yet he believes in Christ and says, "Hallelujah,
Jesus is mine, and I am His!" Don't you believe that this
person is justified already? Though you may read a great
dictionary defining justification by faith, if you have
never enjoyed Christ as a Person, you could never be
justified. Justification is not a matter of a teaching; it
is a Person. We are constituted righteous not by a
teaching, but by a Person. Hallelujah! Christ is our
justification. By receiving Him, we are constituted righteous.

RESURRECTION BY A MAN

First Corinthians 15:21 tells us that by man came
death, and by man came also the resurrection of the
dead. Resurrection came by the man Jesus. We have

already seen many items which come to us through the humanity of Jesus. The destruction of the old serpent, the blessing upon all the people, grace abounding with all its gifts, being constituted righteous, and the resurrection from the dead all come to us by the humanity of Jesus.

SATAN DESTROYED

Satan on the one hand has been bruised and destroyed on the cross, yet on the other hand he is still here making trouble. As human beings, we are under the damaging influence of Satan. How can we destroy this damaging serpent? There is only one way—by feeding on the humanity of Jesus! If we enjoy and eat His humanity, the serpent is destroyed. In John 6:57 the Lord says, "he who eats Me shall also live because of Me." The word "eat" in this verse is a special word, a word which is different from the other words used in this chapter for eating. One version translates this word as "masticate." This means to chew finely, to eat bit by bit in a slow and fine way. We have to eat the Lord, and sometimes we need to masticate Him. This is not to eat roughly, but bit by bit. When we eat too fast, our digestion is impaired. So we must learn to masticate the Lord's humanity. If we eat Him in this way, the old serpent will be nailed to the cross again. This kind of masticating will bruise the head of the serpent. We need to feast on Jesus as the man.

THE BLESSING
ON THOSE AROUND US

In Jesus all the nations are blessed, and through us as Christians, the people around us should also be blessed. But is this our real situation? God told Abraham that through Christ all the nations would be blessed. Thus, as a Christian, we should bring God's blessing upon the people surrounding us. Many times, however, the people around us are not blessed but cursed. Is our wife or husband blessed through us, or cursed through us? This

is the real problem. If we are feeding on the humanity of
Jesus, surely we will bring God's blessing to those around
us.

In 1938, I was told a story concerning a sister who
really loved the Lord. Her husband had accused us
exceedingly because she, since she became a Christian,
neglected her family. She was too busy "preaching Christ."
Her husband was not yet a Christian and was a professor
in one of the largest universities in China. When I
contacted some of the brothers and sisters about this
sister, they all told me the same thing. The sister told
them that now she was just for Jesus; she was not for
her husband or her children. It was clear that this sister
had never tasted the humanity of Christ. At that time I
did not see the light of the enjoyment of Jesus' humanity,
so I told her that she needed to be balanced a little. She
needed to be balanced like the fine flour. If today,
however, the same problem were to come to me, I would
tell them to go home and pray-read all the verses from
Luke on the humanity of Jesus. Then they would know
what they must do and what kind of wife or husband,
mother or father they must be.

On the one hand, the Lord said to His mother that
He was wholly for His heavenly Father. Yet on the other
hand, He went down with His parents and subjected
Himself to them (Luke 2:49-51). This is the humanity of
the Lord Jesus. It is through this kind of humanity that
the people around us can be blessed. I am afraid that the
neighbors living around us are not blessed because we
are like "angels." We do not have the proper humanity.
We all need to be human, but not human in a natural
way. We need the humanity of Jesus. The more we behave
like an angel, the more people around us will be cursed.
But the more we live as proper human beings, the more
people around us will be blessed.

In 1938 another sister in China also came to me
asking, "What can I do with my husband? He will not
believe in the Lord Jesus. I have prayed for him, and I
have talked to him much about the Lord. But the more

I have talked, the more he has gone away." Then I discovered that she was very much like an angel, so I asked her to adjust herself a little and be an ordinary wife to her husband. I assured her that if she would be adjusted, her husband would be saved. Not long after that I received a letter from her telling that her husband had been saved.

God never entrusted His gospel of grace to the angels. Only human beings are qualified to preach the gospel. An angel could tell Cornelius to send for a man named Peter, but that angel was not able to speak a word about the gospel (Acts 10:3-5). Angels are not qualified to preach the gospel; only man is qualified. We must be human to preach the gospel, but we must not be human according to our natural self—that is devilish. We need another category of humanity, the humanity of Jesus. By His humanity we can bring the blessing of God upon all those around us. Wherever we are—in our offices, in our schools, on the campuses, in the neighborhoods, in our families—we can cause all of the people to be much blessed if we will take the humanity of Jesus. Then the gospel will be prevailing.

THE SUPPLY OF THE LORD'S HUMANITY

Now we must go on to see the supply of the Lord's humanity in Hebrews 2. "Since therefore the children have partaken of blood and flesh, He also Himself in like manner shared in the same, that through death He might destroy him who has the might of death, that is, the Devil; and might release those who through fear of death through all their life were held in slavery. For assuredly He does not take hold of angels, but He takes hold of the seed of Abraham. Wherefore He ought to be made like His brothers in all things, that He might become a merciful and faithful High Priest in things pertaining to God, to make propitiation for the sins of the people. For in that He has suffered, being tried, He is able to help those who are being tried" (Heb. 2:14-18).

The Lord Jesus partook of our blood and flesh that

He might destroy the Devil who has the might of death. The deliverance is here, the propitiation is here, and the help is here. The word "help" is not adequate. In Greek it means to support, to render a certain kind of aid, or to supply. If we masticate the humanity of Jesus all the time, it will afford us a kind of aid, help, and supply. Whatever we need, we will receive. Jesus is able to succor those who are being tempted.

Christians today have the religious concept that Jesus is the almighty Savior, yet they do not realize that He is so human, and they do not know how to appreciate His humanity. But of all the offerings, the meal offering is the most important. Only this offering can satisfy God and be a kind of memorial to Him, and only this offering can afford a living for the priesthood. We need to see something of Christ as the meal offering. This matter is greatly neglected in today's Christianity. May the Lord recover the proper humanity of Jesus. This is all we need today. So many Christians have been praying for power from on high, but look at their situation. Perhaps five years ago they received the so-called power from on high, but what about their life today? Even this power didn't deliver them from their temper. It seems the more we look to the Lord as the mighty Savior to deliver us from our temper, the more temper we have. The Lord Jesus will hardly answer this kind of prayer. But if we simply learn to enjoy Christ as the meal offering and masticate His humanity all day long, we will see what will happen to our temper. We will receive succor, aid, support, and supply from the humanity of Jesus.

THE SHORTAGE
OF THE PROPER HUMANITY

Medical doctors tell us that if we have a certain kind of disease, it indicates that we are short of life supply or vitamins. If you are short of life supply, surely you will have a kind of disease. In my native country, there was a village where the people seemed to lose their sight in the evenings. This was because of a kind of disease.

They had no knowledge concerning vitamins to realize that they had a shortage of vitamin A, but they lived on the seashore and caught great quantities of a certain kind of fish. When they began to eat the liver of that fish, they were healed. Of course, we know today that that kind of fish liver is very high in vitamin A. The point is this: if we are short of vitamin A and lose our sight, and then we kneel down to pray to the almighty Savior to heal us, it will not work. The more we pray in that way, the more we will lose our sight. We simply need to eat a large amount of a certain kind of fish liver. What is the "fish liver" for us today? That is the meal offering, the humanity of Jesus.

To lose our temper easily is a kind of disease. It comes from the shortage of Christ's humanity. If we will masticate the humanity of Jesus just like the people in that village ate the fish liver, we will be healed spontaneously. It is so clear in the Bible that we need the Lord's humanity as our meal offering. But we have not seen it. We have been reading the Scriptures for years, and still we have not seen it, simply because we are veiled by our natural concepts. We must forget our natural concepts and come to the pure Word without any kind of religious understanding. If we do this, we will see the importance of Christ's humanity in the Bible.

A MAN IN HEAVEN

Some Christians tried to argue with me in the past, saying it is wrong to tell people that Christ is in heaven as a man. They said that Christ was a man only up to the time when He was crucified. Then after being resurrected, He was no longer a man. Those were preachers who said that they believed in the Bible word by word. So I replied, "What about Acts 7:55-56, where Stephen, while he was being stoned, looked up and saw Jesus as the Son of Man in the heavens? My Jesus, according to the Bible, is still a man in the heavens. And what about the time when the high priest asked Jesus at the judgment whether He was the Son of God? Jesus told him that he would see the Son of Man sitting at the right hand of God in the heavens, and that he would also see the Son of Man coming back in the clouds (Matt. 26:63-64). Of course, there was nothing they could say to such Scriptures. And I must add today that we will see the Son of Man for eternity. In the New Jerusalem, Jesus is there as the Lamb. For the Lord to be the Lamb, He must have the humanity. The Son of God, without His humanity, could never be the Lamb. When He became flesh and dwelt among us, He was called the Lamb of God. The Lamb always has something to do with the matter of incarnation. If He were not incarnated as a man, how could He be the Lamb of God? In eternity, He will be the Son of Man forever.

THE SON OF MAN IN THE MIDST
OF THE CHURCHES

In Revelation 1:13 John saw a vision of the Son of Man in the midst of the local churches. "And in the midst of the lampstands One like the Son of Man, clothed with a garment reaching to the feet, and girded about the breasts with a golden girdle." After the Lord's resurrection and ascension, John saw Him walking in the midst of the local churches as the Son of Man. We all need His humanity.

I have the full assurance that if we will spend our time to enjoy Christ in His humanity, all the local churches will be so bright and shining, practical and real. Christ did not reveal Himself to John as the Son of God. He is the Son of God, but He did not come in that way. He came in the form of the Son of Man. This shows us that the Son of Man is for the local churches. All the local churches need the humanity of Jesus. We must take Him as our food, enjoy Him, and masticate His humanity all the time. We must even pray, "O Lord Jesus, You are the real man, and You are the food of the priesthood. You are the fine flour with which we make the meal offering to bring to the tent of meeting as a present to God the Father." We will see that even to pray in this way will make a difference; there will be the nourishment. We will be nourished with His humanity, and this nourishing will swallow up all our weaknesses. The humanity of Jesus will make us spiritually healthy. If you do not believe me, put it into practice and see. When you are going to lose your temper, just say, "O Lord Jesus, I take Your humanity. I am going to lose my temper, but I take Your humanity, Lord." Then you will see what will happen to your temper.

DIVINITY AND HUMANITY

I am sure that we all have seen the difference between Hebrews chapter one and chapter two. Chapter one shows us that Christ is the Son of God; it even mentions that He is God Himself. Chapter one tells us of His divinity, but chapter two speaks of His humanity. In chapter one, He is God, but in chapter two, He is man. It is at the end of chapter two that we find the succor, aid, support, help, and supply. This comes not so much from Jesus as the Son of God, but from the humanity of Jesus. The man Jesus is the succoring One; He is the aiding One; He is the supporting One; and He is the supplying One. Our help and support come mainly from His humanity. His divinity may be sufficient to succor and supply some angels, but to succor and supply us, He must have His humanity. If we are going to enjoy His succoring, we must feed upon His humanity. This is the meal offering.

Many of you have been in Christianity for years. But according to your realization, was there any meal offering in the so-called Christian service? Was there any nourishment from the humanity of Jesus in those services? From my experience, I can tell you that there was nothing but words. There was no meal offering. Even among the local churches I feel that we do not have enough of the meal offering. We must look to the Lord for His mercy that from now on, in all the meetings, what we present to God would be mainly the meal offering. We must bring something of our experience of the humanity of Jesus to the meetings. Then our meetings will be so enriched, and we will be nourished in a priestly way to have the real priesthood.

BEHOLD THE MAN

Eventually I must say, "Behold the Man." This is what we find in John 19:5: "Then Jesus came out, wearing the thorny crown and the purple garment. And he said to them, Behold the man!" He was crowned then with a crown of thorns, but He is crowned today with a crown of glory. At that time He wore a purple robe, but now He wears a priestly robe. He is crowned with glory and clothed with the priestly robe to care for all the local churches. So, "Behold the Man!" We all need to see this Man, for this Man is our aid, our help, our support, our supply, and our all. This Man is our food for the priesthood.

Chapter Nine

THE MEAL OFFERING FOR THE STANDING BOARDS

Scripture Reading: Exo. 25:8, 9, 10a, 11; 26:15, 29; John 1:14a; Rev. 21:2, 3; 1 Tim. 3:15, 16; 1 Pet. 2:4, 5; Eph. 2:15; 4:24

After pray-reading the above verses, we can realize how much the church is something of humanity. The church is in need of the proper humanity. Many Christians talk only about spirituality when they talk about the church. But these verses show how necessary the proper humanity is in the church life.

THE ARK OF ACACIA WOOD

From the types in the Scriptures we can see the need of a proper humanity for the church life. We have seen in the past what the ark and the tabernacle signify: the ark is Christ, and the tabernacle is the enlargement of the ark. So the tabernacle signifies the enlargement of Christ. This enlargement of Christ is His Body, the church, which is His fullness. When Christ as the ark is increased and enlarged, there is the tabernacle. Then we have the church. Just as the tabernacle is the enlargement of the ark, so the church is the increase and enlargement of Christ.

This can be proved since the ark was made of acacia wood overlaid within and without with gold. "And they shall make an ark of acacia wood...And thou shalt overlay it with pure gold, within and without shalt thou overlay it, and shalt make upon it a crown of gold round

about" (Exo. 25:10a, 11). The gold was made into a type
of crown round about the four sides of the top of the ark.
By the word "crown" we realize that the gold was mainly
for decoration. It is not called the ark of gold, but the ark
of acacia wood. So the main and basic structure of the
ark is wood. Wood in typology always signifies humanity,
and acacia wood typifies the humanity of Jesus. Gold,
which in typology signifies the divine nature, overlays the
wood, which is the human nature. So Christ as the ark
is the human nature overlaid with the divine nature.

As we look at the life of Jesus in the four Gospels, we
see a real man. He was born of a mother. He was a real,
solid, physical man. But in the Gospels, some asked, "Who
is this man?" He was a real man, but there was something
extraordinary about Him. Of course, this was the overlaying gold, His divinity. He was overlaid with the divinity
of God. He was a human with humanity, but this humanity was overlaid with divinity. One day, on the top of a
mountain, He was transfigured. At that time the shining
of the gold was made manifest. It was the outshining of
His divinity. But the humanity was still there. The man
Jesus was there with the shining nature of His divinity.
Jesus was the ark made with acacia wood and overlaid
with the shining gold. The most interesting aspect of this
Jesus is not the gold, but the wood, not primarily His
divinity, but His humanity. This is Jesus as the ark.

THE BOARDS OF THE TABERNACLE

We must also consider the tabernacle. The tabernacle
is mainly composed of forty-eight boards. These boards
are made of the same material and in the same way as
the ark. "And thou shalt make the boards for the
tabernacle of acacia wood, standing up...And thou shalt
overlay the boards with gold" (Exo. 26:15, 29a). The ark
was made with acacia wood overlaid with gold, and the
boards of the tabernacle were also made with the same
material and in the same way—acacia wood overlaid with
gold.

However we must note what Exodus 26:15 says concerning the boards of the tabernacle. In this verse God says that the boards are to be standing up. We all know that gold is valuable, weighty, and shining, but in a sense gold is not capable of standing by itself. In order for the boards of the tabernacle to stand up, there is the need of the acacia wood. Acacia wood is quite adequate for standing up.

So in the tabernacle, again the acacia wood is the main structure. This means that the enlargement of Christ, the church, is composed mainly of the humanity of Jesus overlaid with divinity. We need humanity, and we also need divinity, but it is the humanity in the church that causes the church to stand up. As we look at today's situation, we see that in so many places the so-called Christian churches are not standing up, but rather falling down. Some have even fallen already. They may say they are spiritual, but they are spiritual lying down, not standing up. They are short of the acacia wood, the proper humanity of the man Jesus. Both the ark and the tabernacle had the acacia wood as their main substance. Just as Christ stood by the proper humanity, so His humanity alone can cause the church to stand.

In John 1:14, the word "dwelt" can be translated as "tabernacled." "The Word was made flesh, and tabernacled among us." The Word who was God became flesh and tabernacled among us. We cannot separate the tabernacle from the flesh. If God would tabernacle among us, He needs flesh. So He was made flesh and then tabernacled among us. Without the flesh, it would truly be difficult for God to tabernacle among us. Therefore, in a sense, the flesh is the tabernacle. And the flesh is the humanity. Of course, the flesh here does not mean the evil flesh, but the proper, pure, uplifted flesh. For God to tabernacle among us, there is the need of this flesh.

From John 1:14, we can see that Jesus is this tabernacle. And if we go on from John to the book of Revelation, not only is Jesus Himself the tabernacle, but

He is also the church, the New Jerusalem. "And I saw the holy city, New Jerusalem, coming down out of heaven from God, prepared as a bride adorned for her husband. And I heard a loud voice out of the throne, saying, Behold, the tabernacle of God is with men, and He shall tabernacle with them, and they shall be His peoples, and God Himself shall be with them" (Rev. 21:2, 3). The New Jerusalem is composed mainly of precious stones, something transformed from God's creation. Surely this signifies humanity. The ultimate tabernacle, the New Jerusalem, which is the ultimate consummation of the church, is built up with a proper humanity, the humanity of Jesus.

GOD MANIFEST
IN THE FLESH

Now we need to read 1 Timothy 3:15-16. These two verses in the Scriptures are wonderful and far beyond our understanding. "But if I delay, that you may know how one ought to conduct himself in the house of God, which is the church of the living God, the pillar and base of the truth. And confessedly, great is the mystery of godliness, Who was manifested in the flesh, vindicated in the Spirit, seen by angels, preached among the nations, believed on in the world, taken up in glory." The church is the church of the living God. The church is not just the church of God in heaven or the church in doctrine. It is the church of the living God. The church must have God living in it, and this church of the living God is the pillar and base of the reality.

The architecture used during the time 1 Timothy was written was mainly that of Greece. Greek architecture utilized columns or pillars, which supported the entire building. The church of the living God is just like such pillars with a base to hold Christ as the reality. The word "truth" in verse 15 can also be translated as "reality." For the church to be such a pillar to hold Christ as the reality, the proper humanity of Jesus is required. This is shown in the following verse, where we are told that God was manifested in the flesh. As we have seen, the flesh is simply humanity. This proves that for the church to be the proper pillar to support Christ as the reality, the humanity of Jesus is required.

But 1 Timothy 3:16 does not refer only to Christ. If we read the whole verse carefully, we will see this. It says that God was manifested in the flesh, vindicated in the Spirit, seen by angels, preached to the nations, believed on in the world, and taken up in glory. It seems that the Apostle Paul made a mistake. Was Christ taken up in glory before the preaching to the Gentiles or after? We all know that He was taken up before He was preached. Yet this verse plainly states that Christ is first preached, then believed on, and then taken up in glory. I believe that by now we are all clear. This Christ includes not only the Head, but also the Body. As the Head, He was taken up in glory *before* being preached to the Gentiles. But His Body will be taken up in glory *after* the preaching. By this we see that the manifestation of God in Christ is not only a matter of Christ the Head, but also a matter of His Body, the church. God was manifested in the flesh with Christ, and God is being manifested in the flesh with the church. This is not just the individual person of Christ; this is the person of Christ plus the corporate Christ. Regarding the person of Christ, He was taken up before the preaching. But regarding the corporate Christ, He will be taken up in glory after the preaching. Therefore, by putting these two verses together, we can see what the church is. The church is just the manifestation of God in Christ. This depends very much on the humanity of Jesus.

According to our religious concept, the word "flesh" has a bad connotation. Whenever we speak about the flesh, we mean something degraded. Of course, our flesh is not good, but the flesh of Jesus is much better than ours. We do not appreciate our flesh because it is so poor and sinful, but we have another flesh. The flesh of Jesus is wonderful! This is His perfect humanity. Hence, for the church to manifest God, we need the humanity of Jesus. We need to take His humanity. I am so happy for this verse that says God was manifest, not in the Spirit, but in the flesh.

God manifest in the flesh is seen by angels and preached to the Gentiles. We are preaching not only Christ, but Christ with the church. How could we preach the Head without the Body? Have you ever seen a person without a body? If you were to come into the meeting without your body, you would be a monster. But this is exactly what many poor Christians are preaching today. They preach only about Christ the Head. We are preaching Christ with His Body. Christ and the church are the great mystery of God (Eph. 5:32). This is what must be preached unto the Gentiles. Eventually this corporate Christ will be taken up in glory. This is the church life. Yet for this church life we need the proper humanity. Neither American flesh, Chinese flesh, Japanese flesh, nor any other flesh is good for the church life. Only Jesus' flesh will do. For the church we need the humanity of Jesus.

Confessedly, great is the mystery of godliness, that is, God manifest in the flesh. Can we imagine this: God is manifest in the flesh? God has no intention to manifest Himself in angels. God does not love them so much; they are simply His servants. God loves the church, so He became manifest in the flesh. This is Christ and the church, the great mystery of God.

THE SPIRITUAL HOUSE,
THE PRIESTHOOD

The next point that we must see is in 1 Peter. Here the Apostle Peter tells us that Christ is the living stone, and we are the living stones. "To whom coming, as unto a living stone, disallowed indeed of men, but chosen of God, and precious. Ye also, as living stones, are built up a spiritual house, a holy priesthood, to offer up spiritual sacrifices, acceptable to God by Jesus Christ" (1 Pet. 2:4, 5, lit.). We know that stones in the Bible signify material for building. Christ is the living stone, and we are the living stones to be built into a spiritual house. This spiritual house is the priesthood. I appreciate the King James Version in this verse. It puts a comma after "spiritual house" to show that the spiritual house is the priesthood. "Ye also, as living stones, are built up a spiritual house, a holy priesthood...." This proves that the priesthood is the spiritual house, and the spiritual house is the priesthood.

In 1966, when we covered the matter of the priesthood (*The Stream,* Vol. 5, No. 4 through Vol. 6, No. 4), we pointed out that in the New Testament, the word "priesthood" has two different meanings. First, it means the priestly service or priestly ministry. Second, it means a priestly body or a body of priests. In English there is only one word, but in Greek there are two different words with these two different meanings. In Hebrews 7, the word "priesthood" signifies the priestly service or office. But the word for "priesthood" in 1 Peter means the priestly body or body of priests. The spiritual house is not the priestly service, but a priestly body. It is a corporate entity. The priests built up together are the spiritual house. This is the meaning of the word "priesthood" here.

The priesthood in the New Testament is different from that mentioned in the Old Testament. In the New Testament, the priests built up together are the tabernacle. They are the spiritual house. In the typology of the Old Testament, it is rather difficult to put these two together. Hence, in the type, the tabernacle and the priests are two categories of things. Actually these two categories typify one thing in two aspects, that is, God's building which is the tabernacle, the house of God. This house is built up with the priests who are the living stones. We are the priesthood, and we are the living stones. When we are built up together, we become a body of priests, and this is the priesthood.

THE DIET
OF THE PRIESTHOOD

In Leviticus, we see that the priests lived mainly on the meal offering. Their entire existence depended principally upon the meal offering. The priests are the boards of the tabernacle standing up, and they exist by feeding on the meal offering, which is just the fine humanity of Jesus. Today as the priests, we are the boards of the tabernacle, but to stand up we must feed on the humanity of Jesus. It is not enough to feed on Jesus as the Passover Lamb or as the heavenly manna. Feeding on Jesus as the heavenly manna is only sufficient to maintain us in the wilderness. To be the standing boards in the tabernacle, we need the humanity of Jesus as our daily food.

Suppose that not one of the Israelites offered the meal offering, and the priests did not receive anything as a meal offering. This would put the priests upon a starvation diet; they would not have their proper food. The food of the priests is not ordinary food, but quite extraordinary; it is the meal offering. If in the church there is a shortage of enjoying Christ's humanity, the local church will be extremely weak. If all the members enjoy Christ merely as the slain Lamb and as the heavenly manna, but do not enjoy Him as the meal offering, all the boards will not be standing but fallen.

We may have some knowledge of the Bible, and we may have some gifts; we may even have a certain measure of spirituality; but if we are not enjoying the humanity of Jesus, we are simply fallen. We have nothing which is able to support us. The only thing that can make us stand up is the humanity of Jesus. This has been lost and neglected by Christianity for centuries, but I do believe the Lord is going to recover it. This is what is needed for the church life. The tabernacle is composed mainly of the boards, and the boards are the priests, who can exist only by feeding on the meal offering. We are the priests, the boards, the materials for building up the local church. We do need something to feed on in order to stand up—this is the humanity of Jesus which is the meal offering.

Let me illustrate again. Suppose all the Israelites had offered only the burnt offering, the peace offering, the sin offering, and the trespass offering, without presenting the meal offering. I do believe many priests would have starved. This is the situation of today's Christians. They appreciate the Lord's death on the cross as the sin and trespass offering; they enjoy peace with God through Christ as the peace offering; but they have no experience of the meal offering. They simply do not have this kind of apprehension or understanding. This is why there is little building up of the church among Christians today.

The church is the house of God. It is today's tabernacle and is composed of the boards standing up. The standing boards are the priests, who can exist only by feeding on the meal offering. This means that for us to be the boards for the building up of God's tabernacle, we must feed on the humanity of Christ. Without the meal offering, there can be no standing boards for the tabernacle, and the whole tabernacle will fall apart. This is the situation today. We may have the burnt offering, the peace offering, the sin offering, and the trespass offering, but without the meal offering we have nothing to support the priests who are the standing boards. The real support is the priestly food of the meal offering. Only the humanity of Jesus is the priestly food capable of supporting the priests as the standing boards. We all must pray that we may experience and masticate the humanity of Jesus. We will then have something of His humanity to bring into the meeting and present to God as the meal offering. This meal offering will be the priestly food to so many priests among us, enabling them to become the standing boards. Something will then be built up as the tabernacle, and God will have a dwelling place.

ONE NEW MAN

Eventually we come to the new man in the book of Ephesians. To see this new man we must read both Ephesians 2:15 and 4:24. "Having abolished in His flesh the law of commandments in ordinances, that He might create the two in Himself into one new man, making peace...And have put on the new man, which according to God was created in righteousness and holiness of the truth." The church is a new man, and as a man it requires the proper humanity, the new humanity, which is just Christ. We must put on the new man, which means we must put on the humanity of Jesus.

Ephesians 2:15 says that Christ has already created the new man, and then Ephesians 4:24 tells us to put on the new man. Let me illustrate it in this way: Christ has already accomplished redemption, but we must apply this redemption to ourselves. This means we must put on His redemption. If anyone would not apply or put on this redemption, it will not affect him in any way. It is the same principle with the new man. The new man has been created, but we need to put on the new man and apply to ourselves what Christ has created on the cross. The way to put on the new man is simply to enjoy the humanity of Jesus. By partaking of the humanity of Jesus day by day, we are putting on the new man.

Chapter Ten

THE UNITING POWER FOR
THE CHURCH LIFE

Scripture Reading: Exo. 26:26-29; Luke 15:22; Eph. 1:13b; 4:2, 3; Acts 16:6, 7

We have seen how the tabernacle was composed of wooden boards overlaid with gold. It is so clear that the tabernacle did not stand by the gold, but by the wood. Wood was the main element which enabled the tabernacle to stand, and the wood was even the main element of the tabernacle. Gold provided decoration, beauty, value, and preciousness, but wood provided the standing power. Wood is a type of the humanity of Jesus, indicating that the standing power of the church, today's tabernacle, is the humanity of Jesus. If we are lacking the humanity of Jesus, the church will be very weak and will have no power to stand. The church must have acacia wood as the humanity of Jesus for its standing power.

THE UNITING BARS

In the tabernacle there were not only the boards, but also the bars. "Thou shalt make bars of acacia wood; five for the boards of the one side of the tabernacle, and five bars for the boards of the other side of the tabernacle, and five bars for the boards of the side of the tabernacle, for the two sides westward. And the middle bar in the midst of the boards shall reach from end to end. And thou shalt overlay the boards with gold, and make their rings of gold for holders for the bars: and thou shalt overlay the bars with gold" (Exo. 26:26-29, lit.).

The tabernacle had twenty standing boards on one side and twenty standing boards on the other side. Then at the rear, on the west side, there were eight standing boards. Altogether, there were forty-eight separate boards standing up in the tabernacle. How then could these forty-eight boards be one? How could they be united? This is the function of the bars. If we enjoy the humanity of Jesus we become strong standing boards, but we may not be united with other boards. We are enabled to stand, but we are not united. This is why we need the uniting bars. The uniting bars were also made of acacia wood overlaid with gold. But the rings for the bars were made of solid gold.

All forty-eight boards were standing up, but it was the bars which held them together. Exodus 26:26-29 tells us clearly that on each of the three sides of the tabernacle, there were five bars, with the middle bar reaching from end to end. If then the middle bar was one long bar going from end to end, where were the other four bars? It must be that the first bar was above the middle bar, but it only extended halfway across. Then the second bar continued above the middle bar to complete the other half. The fourth bar must have gone halfway across below the middle bar, and the fifth continued the other half at the bottom. So there were five bars on every side, with the middle bar going from end to end. Since the middle bar extended from end to end, we can realize that the other four bars must be arranged in this way. Otherwise, there could be no middle bar. Thus we have the number five, since there are five bars, and we have the number three, because there are three layers of the bars.

THE GOLDEN RINGS

On each side of the tabernacle, the bars united the boards. But simply to have the boards and the bars was not sufficient; there was also the need of the rings. The golden rings were on the overlaying gold of the boards. Each board was overlaid with gold, and on the overlaying gold of each board there were three solid gold rings. Thus, there were at least 144 rings for the fifteen bars on the three sides of the tabernacle. When the boards, the bars, and the rings were all joined together, there was the unity. All forty-eight boards united together became one dwelling place.

According to typology, the uniting bars are the Holy Spirit, and the rings for the bars are also the Holy Spirit. Both are types of the Holy Spirit. Why are these two things, the rings and the bars, necessary to signify the one Holy Spirit? This requires the proper experience as well as the proper verses for confirmation. The last part of Ephesians 1:13 says, "In Whom also believing, you were sealed with the Holy Spirit of the promise." This is the initial experience of the Holy Spirit. Once a person believes in the Lord Jesus, he is sealed with the Holy Spirit. But in the same book, Ephesians 4:3, we read, "Being diligent to keep the oneness of the Spirit in the uniting bond of peace." This verse does not have the word "Holy" before Spirit. We must just keep the unity of the Spirit. There is a significant reason for this, which we see later. Of course, some may say that the Spirit *is* the Holy Spirit, and I agree. But do not think that the Apostle Paul was careless with his words. There is a purpose in his using "Holy Spirit" in Ephesians 1:13, and "the Spirit" in Ephesians 4:3.

THE DIFFERENCE BETWEEN
THE RINGS AND THE BARS

What is the difference between the sealing of the Holy Spirit and the keeping of the unity of the Spirit? To receive the sealing of the Holy Spirit is easy. Once we believe, we have it. But to keep the unity of the Spirit is not as easy. After having it, we need to keep it. If I were to ask if you have the sealing of the Holy Spirit, you would answer, "Amen." But are you keeping the unity of the Spirit? That is another matter. There may be three brothers who all believe in the Lord Jesus; therefore, they are sealed with the Holy Spirit. But since they live together in the same house, they are fighting all the time. Do you think they are keeping the unity of the Spirit?

The Apostle Paul wrote Ephesians 1:13 in the past tense: "In Whom also believing, you were sealed." This has already been accomplished. But in chapter four, he says, "Being diligent to keep the oneness of the Spirit." They have something, yet they lack something. They have been sealed with the Holy Spirit, but they are short of being diligent to keep the oneness of the Spirit. Thus we see that the sealing of the Holy Spirit is an initial experience, but keeping the oneness of the Spirit is something of further growth and improvement. We all have the sealing of the Holy Spirit. This occurs at the beginning of our Christian life. It is without condition or terms, for it is an accomplished fact. But keeping the oneness of the Spirit depends upon certain conditions. You may have it, and I may not have it. I may have it now, but I may not have it later. You may have it today, but you may not have it tomorrow.

Keeping the oneness of the Spirit is a great improvement from the sealing of the Holy Spirit. It is still one Spirit, but in two stages. In the first stage of our Christian life, the Holy Spirit is the sealing Spirit. But we must go on from the first stage to the second in order to experience the Spirit of the uniting bars.

In the first stage, the Holy Spirit is just a ring. In ancient times, a ring was used as a seal. Even today some still use a ring as a seal. Every item of the tabernacle in Exodus has a spiritual meaning. The golden rings on the boards are a type of the sealing Spirit. The Holy Spirit is the golden ring that seals us. After we were saved, we were sealed with the Holy Spirit.

This can be seen in the return of the prodigal son in Luke 15. "The father said to his servants, Bring forth the best robe, and put it on him; and put a ring on his hand" (v. 22). The father put a robe on his son, which signifies Christ as his righteousness. But this is not all. He also put a ring on his hand. This is the sealing of the Holy Spirit. The Holy Spirit was given as a seal.

All the boards of the tabernacle had rings, but that alone could not unite them. They needed the uniting bars. Two brothers may be saved and have the sealing of the Holy Spirit, but they may still argue and always act independently of one another. They need lowliness and meekness, longsuffering, and forbearing of one another in love (Eph. 4:2). This cannot come from *their* humanity; it requires another kind of humanity. One version says "making allowances" in place of "forbearing one another." This is why it is necessary to be diligent to keep the oneness of the Spirit in the uniting bond of peace. If these two brothers go on from the first stage of the Spirit to the second, there will be some improvement. Not only will they have experienced the Holy Spirit as the golden rings, but they will also experience Him as the uniting bars. In the first stage, the Holy Spirit was just a ring, purely of gold; there was no wood. But in the second stage, something is added. There is not only gold, but also acacia wood. Instead of one element, there are now two. Hence, to keep the unity, we need the humanity of Jesus.

THE SPIRIT OF JESUS

Many Christians talk about the Holy Spirit or the Spirit of God. But have they ever heard of the Spirit of Jesus? In the whole Bible, only one verse uses this phrase, and the King James Version does not have it. The proper translation of Acts 16:6-7 is this: "Now when they had gone throughout Phrygia and the region of Galatia, and were forbidden of the Holy Spirit to preach the word in Asia, after they were come to Mysia, they assayed to go into Bithynia: but the Spirit of Jesus suffered them not." Many Christians have never heard that the Spirit of God today is also the Spirit of a man. This is because the Spirit today is not only the Spirit of God, but also the Spirit of Jesus. The name Jesus is not a divine title, but the name of a man. Today the Spirit is not only the Spirit of God, but also the Spirit of Jesus. The Spirit of God has only one element, the divinity of the divine nature.

But the Spirit of Jesus has another element, the humanity of Jesus. In this Spirit there is divinity as well as humanity. He is the Spirit of God for He has divinity in Him, and He is also the Spirit of Jesus because humanity is also within Him.

I would now like to quote a few sentences from chapter five of *The Spirit of Christ* by Andrew Murray, entitled, "The Spirit of the Glorified Jesus." He says, "From His nature, as it was glorified in the resurrection and ascension, His Spirit came forth as the Spirit of His human life, glorified into the union with the Divine, to make us partakers of all that He had personally wrought out and acquired, of Himself and His glorified life. And in virtue of His having perfected in Himself a new holy human nature on our behalf, He could now communicate what previously had no existence—a life at once human and Divine. And the Holy Spirit could come down as the Spirit of the God-man—most really the Spirit of God, and yet as truly the spirit of man."

Today the Spirit of Jesus is not only the Spirit of divinity, but also the Spirit of humanity. When we were first saved, we only experienced Him as the divine Spirit with His divinity. But as we grow, we begin to experience Him not only as the Spirit of divinity, but also as the Spirit of humanity. It is in the Spirit of humanity that there is the uniting bar. As the Spirit of divinity, He is the ring that seals us, but as the Spirit of humanity, He is the bar that unites us in the ring.

THE UPLIFTED HUMAN VIRTUES

For the standing up of the church life, we need the humanity of Jesus, and for the uniting, we also need the humanity of Jesus. I have never before seen so clearly why the Apostle Paul put all of these human virtues in Ephesians 4:2-3. He mentions lowliness or humility, meekness or gentleness, longsuffering, and bearing with one another in love. All these are human virtues, and they are all required for keeping the oneness of the Spirit in the uniting bond of peace. They are all related to the oneness of the Spirit. It is not the Holy Spirit or the Spirit of God that is mentioned here, but *the* Spirit, which is the Spirit of man or the Spirit of humanity. He is indeed the Spirit of God, but here He is the Spirit of *humanity*.

We need another illustration in order to be more clear. Suppose there are two brothers who were sick. One had cancer three years ago, and the Lord healed him. The other almost died of a certain disease, but the Lord delivered him. Both of them received a miraculous healing from the Lord. But do you believe these two brothers could ever be united as one because of these miracles? I am afraid that the more they speak about their miracles, the more they will be divided. They need to call: "O Lord Jesus, You are so lowly; You are so meek; You were such a man on this earth. And now, Lord Jesus, You are this man in me. O Lord Jesus, O Lord Jesus!" If these two brothers will learn to call on the Lord in this way, spontaneously they will be one. This experience of the Spirit is the uniting bar, and within the bar is the acacia wood, the humanity of Jesus. The more they talk about their miracles, the more individualistic they will become. But the more they masticate the humanity of the Lord Jesus, the more they will be spontaneously one with each other and with others.

Today the Lord Jesus is the Spirit of humanity; He is the Spirit of a man. His humanity is in the Holy Spirit, just as His divinity is in the Holy Spirit. We all have the golden rings, but we still cannot be one. We need the uniting bars, the Spirit of the man, Jesus. The mighty power of Jesus is in His divinity, but lowliness, meekness, and all His human virtues are in His humanity. It is only by these human virtues that we can keep the oneness of the Spirit in the uniting bond of peace.

I must repeat again that lowliness, meekness, and gentleness are not virtues of divinity, but virtues of humanity. Longsuffering and bearing with one another in love are also human virtues. All of these are in the Spirit of a man. Jesus has uplifted the human nature. Now there is something in the universe which never existed before

His resurrection—the new uplifted human nature of Jesus! This humanity is now an element of the Spirit of Jesus. If we call on His name and feed upon Him, all the virtues of this uplifted human nature will be ours. Then we will be united by His humanity. Only by these experiences can we keep the oneness of the Spirit in the bond of peace.

We do not need to pay so much attention to miracles or to having a victorious life, but we do need to enjoy Jesus as a man. The more we masticate Jesus as a man, the more we will enjoy all the virtues of His humanity. Then the Spirit will become the uniting bars among us. Regardless of how much the brothers take advantage of us, we will make allowances. We are just so willing to bear with one another in love. This is not something of the divine virtues, but of the human virtues. It is by this kind of life that we are spontaneously one. We are united by the bars of acacia wood overlaid with gold.

FIVE BARS IN THREE LAYERS

Now we must come back to the five bars which are in three layers on each side of the tabernacle. The number five in the Bible is always composed of four plus one. If we look at our hand, we will see four fingers and one thumb. We never count our fingers three plus two, but always four plus one. If we had three fingers and two thumbs, it would be rather awkward. Moreover, if we had all fingers or all thumbs, it would be worse. God's creation is marvelous. How could anyone say that there is no God? The best designer could not design a hand in such a way. Four in the Bible stands for the creatures; there are four living creatures in Revelation 4:6. One in the Bible signifies the one God. So four plus one means man plus God. We did not have God before we were saved, but now that we are regenerated, we are man plus God. The number five means God plus man to bear responsibility. These five bars are not just for appearance. They are arranged in such a way that they hold the boards together. They bear such a responsibility.

These five bars are in three layers. This signifies resurrection. The Lord Jesus was resurrected on the third day. We are man plus God, but in resurrection. It is not in the natural disposition, but in resurrection. Furthermore, there are not only three layers of bars, but also three sides to the tabernacle. This signifies the Triune God. Hence, we have man plus God in resurrection with the three Persons of the Triune God. This is how we are united. All forty-eight boards in the tabernacle were united in this way. Since we are the boards today, we must be fully united by taking the humanity of Jesus in resurrection with the Triune God.

The main factor of the uniting power in the church life is the acacia wood within the gold. The unity comes from the humanity of Jesus. Today this humanity is in the Spirit. When we have this Spirit, we have the humanity of Jesus, the resurrection, and the Triune God. All of these matters are related to the humanity of Jesus. If we simply enjoy His humanity, we will have the resurrection with the Triune God. May we look to the Lord that all of these things may be put into practice in our daily lives.

CHAPTER ELEVEN

THE HUMANITY OF JESUS AND GIFTS TO THE BODY

Scripture Reading: Psa. 68:18; Eph. 4:7, 8, 11-16

The previous seven chapters on the meal offering cover five major points. The first point concerns the significance of the meal offering. We have seen that the meal offering is a present to God of the humanity of Jesus which we have experienced, enjoyed, and appreciated. Second, the meal offering constitutes worship to God. Third, the meal offering affords priestly food for the priesthood. Fourth, the meal offering not only constitutes worship to God and affords food for the priesthood, but also produces standing boards, which are the main structure of God's dwelling place. By feeding on the meal offering, all the priests become the standing boards. Fifth, the meal offering forms the tabernacle by uniting all the boards together.

GIFTED PERSONS

The sixth point is very deep and difficult to explain. It is perhaps the deepest aspect of the meal offering; it concerns the making of the gifts. The gifts in Ephesians 4 are not abilities, but the gifted persons, such as the apostles, the prophets, the evangelists, and the shepherds and teachers. These are not skills or abilities; these are persons gifted with skills and abilities. Moreover, Ephesians 4:11-16 reveals that not only are the apostles, prophets, evangelists, and shepherds and teachers gifts to the Body, but every member of the Body is a gift.

Consider your own body. Every member of your body

is a gift to your body. Do not think that only Paul the Apostle was a gift to the Body and you are not. Perhaps Paul was an arm, but you may be at least a little finger. The arm is a gift to the body. Regardless of how small we are, even less than the least, we are still gifts to the Body. Ephesians 4 speaks of the effectual working in the measure of *every* part. Each of us is at least one of many parts, and all the parts are gifts.

CONSTITUTED A GIFT

We must see how all the gifts are made or constituted. When Paul was Saul of Tarsus, he was not a gift. He was a persecutor, an enemy, of the Body. After he was saved, however, he became a gift. But "became" is not an adequate word. It is better to say that after he was saved, he was constituted a gift. He was a rebel, a foe, an enemy, and a persecutor to the Body, but he was constituted an apostle. To be constituted means to be composed or transfigured with additional elements added in. Without the adding of these elements, nothing can be constituted. Paul was a rebel, but an element was added into this rebel which killed the rebellious germs. Other elements were also added which built him up as an apostle.

The point we must see is that the main element by which Paul was constituted an apostle is the humanity of Jesus. To prove this we must read Psalm 68:18 with an improved rendering: "Thou hast ascended on high, thou led a train of vanquished foes: thou hast received gifts in man; yea, for the rebellious also, that the Lord God might dwell among them." Christ ascended on high, and having conquered all His enemies, He led captive a corporate train of vanquished foes, including Paul the Apostle. Then He received gifts in *man* and for man, even for the rebellious man. He received the gifts in His *humanity* for our rebellious humanity. So in this verse we see two kinds of humanities: the humanity of Jesus, by which He received the gifts, and our rebellious humanity, for which He received the gifts.

FROM REBEL TO APOSTLE

I believe we all know how Christ made such a rebel as Saul of Tarsus into an apostle. He persecuted Stephen, and he persecuted others in Jerusalem, but he was not satisfied. Therefore, he went to the high priests and obtained authority to go to Damascus and bind all those who called on the name of the Lord. While he was journeying, a light shone from heaven, and he fell to the earth. The Lord asked him, "Saul, Saul, why are you persecuting me?" When Saul asked who He was, the Lord replied that He was Jesus, the One whom he was persecuting. From that moment, something of the ascended Jesus entered into that rebel. He was so clever, able to see everything, but after Jesus came into him, he became blind. He could see nothing. Many of us need to be blind. When Jesus really gets into us, we cannot see anymore. Formerly, Saul was leading others; now others led him (Acts 9).

The constituting of Saul into an apostle proceeded from that day to the time of Acts 13. That rebel was constituted an apostle by Jesus, and he became one of the greatest apostles. But do not think that he became an apostle overnight. Such a constitution required a long time, a long process, for all the elements of the ascended Jesus to be added into Him. Jesus made him an apostle; Jesus constituted him with all His own elements as an apostle. Jesus has received all the saved persons from the Father, and all of these, including Saul, eventually become the gifts. Christ received these gifts in His humanity, and then He gave all of these saved ones to His Body for the perfecting of His Body.

IN MAN

For the making and constituting of a gifted person, the humanity of Jesus is required. Jesus did not do this in His divinity, but in His humanity. He received the gifts in man. Darby's New Translation uses this phrase "in man." The Lord received the gifts as a man, on a man's standing, and in a man's position. After His ascension, He did not receive the gifts in the position of the Son of God, but in the position of man. For Him to receive the gifts means that He constituted the gifts.

When we were saved, Christ received us from the Father. We were called and chosen by God in eternity, so we belonged to the Father. Then the Father passed us on to Jesus. The Father gave, and the Son received. After the Son received us, He sent us, for example, to the church in Los Angeles where we became gifts for the building up of the church. We were chosen, predestinated, and called by the Father, and then given to His Son Jesus. Finally, Jesus gave us to the church in Los Angeles as gifts. But whether these chosen, predestinated, called, and given ones will be proper gifts or not depends upon the constitution of the humanity of Jesus within them. The determining factor is how much of the humanity of Jesus has been wrought into us. The Lord did not receive us in His divinity, but in His humanity. This is very meaningful.

In the past, much has been said concerning the need of the divine life and nature to be wrought into us. But if we spend more time in pray-reading the Word, we will see that God intends to work into us the divine life *with a human nature*. God wants to work Christ into us, and Christ is not only the Son of God, but also the Son of Man. God intends to work a Person into us who has the life of God and the nature of man.

I remember some of the Western missionaries I met years ago in the Far East. Some had doctor's degrees and were excellent preachers, but they were not so useful. Some however, were not learned and had no degree, yet they were very much used by the Lord. At that time I did not understand, but now I know the reason. Those who were more useful in the hands of the Lord were those who were enjoying the humanity of Jesus. It may be that they did not know this term, yet they did in fact participate in the Lord's humanity. Some of the missionaries could not preach and were not able to teach well, but they brought a good number to the Lord by experiencing the humanity of Jesus.

I have seen all kinds of Christians: formal Christians, fundamental Christians, Pentecostal Christians, and inner-life Christians. I have not only seen these different kinds of Christians, but under God's sovereignty I was also among many of them. Yet I must say that all of them do not experience much of the humanity of Jesus. The Pentecostals are supposed to be powerful, and the fundamentalists are supposed to know the Bible well, but eventually they may not be so useful in the hands of God because they are simply short of the humanity of Jesus. They are gifts to the Body, but they have a shortage of the humanity of Jesus.

"JESUSLY" HUMAN

Please do not misunderstand what I mean when I speak of the proper humanity. I realize that some may think that we must simply be human. So they say, "Let us be human. God does not want angels; He wants human beings. Let us go to the beach, engage in sports and watch T.V." That may be human, but not *Jesusly* human. We must be *Jesusly* human, not humanly human. I am not referring to our natural and fallen humanity. We should not bring anything natural into the realm of Jesus. We already have enough of this kind of humanity. We need another category of humanity, a new, holy human nature, as mentioned by Andrew Murray in his book, *The Spirit of Christ*. Jesus perfected such a human nature, not in a natural way, but in a divine way. It is humanity, yet something divine.

Jesus is a man, but His humanity is of a different source than ours. By death and resurrection, He uplifted this humanity. His humanity is not only new and holy, but also uplifted. Our natural humanity can never match His. It may be difficult to discern the difference in word, but in our experience there is a great difference. Our humanity at its best is just a shadow; the humanity of

Jesus is the reality. A genuine flower and an artificial flower look alike in size, color, shape, and form. If you lack discernment, you may say that they are identical. But they are absolutely not. One has come out of life; the other has no element of life.

USEFUL MEMBERS

For the building up of the local church today, we need the standing boards, the uniting bars, and all the members to be the proper gifts by being constituted with the humanity of Jesus. Not only must we be standing up and united, but also we must be useful. Every member among us must be useful. We are all gifts to the Body, so we must function in a useful way. How can this be done? Only by being constituted with the humanity of Jesus.

Years ago I could not speak in this way because I did not have this light. I was not so clear, but I did have some experience. Praise the Lord, today we see that our need is the humanity of Jesus! In the past, we thought that if we had certain kinds of gifts and manifestations with the baptism of the Holy Spirit and if we had a certain amount of Bible knowledge with proper training, then surely we would be useful. This may be of some use, but eventually what we do without Jesus' humanity will be torn down by what we are. Brother Watchman Nee used to tell us that some people build up twelve inches by what they do, but tear down fourteen inches by what they are. This means that they tear down more than they build up. Hence, it is better for them not to do anything. We may build up a certain amount by our Bible doctrine and knowledge, but we will damage more than we build up because of our shortage of the humanity of Jesus. In the church life, we need the humanity of Jesus much more than the gifts, the so-called baptism, or the knowledge of the Bible.

PERFECTING AND EQUIPPING

Ephesians 4:11-12 says that all the gifted persons do not build up the church directly, but indirectly. "He gave some apostles, and some prophets, and some evangelists, and some shepherds and teachers, for the perfecting of the saints unto the work of the ministry, unto the building up of the Body of Christ." All the gifted persons are for the perfecting of others, thus equipping them to be useful members. To perfect and equip is simply to help the saints to grow in life. To perfect and equip the saints is to feed them with the meal offering, the humanity of Jesus.

Suppose we have before us a normal baby with all of its proper organs and members. Many of the members of this little babe do not yet function properly because it is short of growth and maturity. The baby has two feet with legs, but he cannot stand up or walk because he is short of the growth in life. The mother must therefore perfect him and equip him. This is not done by putting many good things upon him. If she went to the supermarket and bought many good things to heap them upon the baby, it would not help. There is only one way for the mother to perfect her baby to maturity—by feeding him. If a baby has proper food, he will grow in life. All his organs and members will mature into useful function.

We are all born priests; we have been born into the priestly family. But we are all priestly babes; we need the growth in life. The main food which will enable us to grow into mature priests is the meal offering, which signifies the humanity of Jesus. This meal offering comes from the labor of the more mature ones. In the church there should be a number of mature ones who labor on the good land to produce the grain for making the meal offering. They must bring this offering to the tent of meeting to present to the Father. The remainder will be the food for feeding the priestly family.

THE PROPER FOOD

Today the Lord Jesus is constituting certain members
of His Body into the proper gifts to the Body, and He is
doing this by the way of His humanity. He has received
gifts in man and in the position of man. Therefore, the
fastest way for us to grow is by feeding on the humanity
of Jesus. It is not by having gifts or Bible knowledge,
although it is not my purpose to oppose these things. The
fastest way for Christians to grow is by feeding upon
Christ's humanity. The more we masticate Jesus, the more
we will grow.

There are many matured ones among Christians today,
but they are not matured in life. They may be matured
in knowledge, in teaching, or in gifts, but as far as life is
concerned, they are babes. Regardless of what kind of
gifts we have, it is exceedingly easy for us to be carried
away and tossed to and fro by the winds of doctrine.
Christians today have all of these things, yet they are
not stable; it is so easy for them to change. This is because
the proper growth in life is lacking.

Do not think that I am criticizing today's Christians.
I am simply stating the facts of today's Christianity. In
Luke 24:49, the Lord likened the baptism of the Holy
Spirit to a piece of clothing. The disciples were told to
wait until they were clothed with power from on high.
But can anyone grow by being clothed? We all know that
clothing is not for growing, but for covering. What is
lacking today is the proper food for the Christians. Gifts
cannot feed us, knowledge cannot feed us, and even the
best capabilities cannot feed us. We may be able to do
many things, but doing cannot feed us. This is why many
Christians are so poor today. They have clothing, knowledge, and capabilities, but they have no food. The food
can come only from the humanity of Jesus. The humanity
of Jesus is the main food for the priests.

Those who bear responsibility in a local church should
not demand so much from the younger ones. Instead, they
must labor on the land, produce the grain, make the flour,

and prepare the meal offering for the tent of meeting. Then the remainder will be for all the priests to feed upon. Thus all the infant priests will grow into useful gifts for the Body. The real need for today's church life is not teachings but the humanity of Jesus. Ephesians 4:15 tells us to hold truth, which means the reality: "But holding to truth in love, we may grow up into Him in all things, Who is the Head, Christ." The reality is mainly in the humanity of Jesus. Jesus is the reality, and we must grow up into Him in everything. We must grow up into the Head in all things in our daily walk by holding the humanity of Jesus. For Christ to receive gifts in man means that we must hold to His humanity in order to enjoy the reality and grow into useful gifts to the Body. As we grow we are able to function. This is why Ephesians 4:16 says that out from the Head the whole Body is fitted and knit together by the joints of supply according to the operation in measure of every part. This makes for the growth of the Body unto the building up of itself in love.

This is the building up of the church. We must all look to the Lord that we may see how the standing boards and the uniting bars are produced, as well as how the gifts are constituted. The only way is by feeding on the humanity of Jesus. It is thus that we will grow in life and be constituted as the proper gifts for the building up of the Body.

CHAPTER TWELVE

THE HUMANITY OF JESUS
FOR THE FLOWING OF LIFE

Scripture Reading: John 7:37-39; Phil. 1:19

In the last chapter we saw how the humanity of Jesus has so much to do with the making and producing of gifted persons. Christ as the Head of the church received all the useful, gifted persons from the Father in the position of man. This simply means that He imparted Himself as such a humanity into the rebellious ones to make them the useful, gifted persons.

Now we come to the seventh point, which is revealed in John 7:37-39: "Now on the last day, the great day of the feast, Jesus stood and cried out, saying, If anyone thirst, let him come to Me and drink. He who believes in Me, as the Scripture said, out of his innermost being shall flow rivers of living water. But this He said concerning the Spirit, Whom those who believed in Him were about to receive; for the Spirit was not yet, because Jesus was not yet glorified."

This portion of the Word is very much related to the humanity of Jesus. We all know these verses well; I believe that many of us can recite them. We pay our attention in these verses mostly to the matter of the living water. And it is clear that the living water is just the Spirit. But we have probably never seen that the Spirit in this passage is much related to the humanity of Jesus. This Spirit, who is the living water flowing from within us, is constituted of the humanity of Jesus. Without the humanity of Jesus, there could never be such a Spirit. This is made clear by verse 39, which says that the Spirit was not yet because Jesus was not yet glorified. This proves that the Spirit was constituted with the glorified humanity of Jesus. We must realize that at this point the Scripture is speaking of a resurrected humanity.

THE SPIRIT OF JESUS

The Spirit mentioned here is different from the Spirit of God. The Spirit of God already existed. We could never say that the Spirit of God was not yet. But the very Spirit mentioned here by the Lord Jesus was not yet. Hence, this Spirit must be something new and different from the Spirit of God. The Spirit of God was constituted only with the divine essence of God. But after the resurrection of Christ, the Spirit was constituted with something more. He not only had the divine essence, but the human essence as well. Formerly, the Spirit of God was constituted with God's essence only, but now the Spirit of Jesus is constituted not only with the essence of God, but also with the essence of a man. Previously, the Spirit had only one element, the divine; now the Spirit of Jesus includes two elements, the divine and the human. Thus, before Jesus was glorified, which means before He was resurrected, the Spirit of Jesus was not yet. The Spirit with the divine essence was there, but the Spirit with both the divine and human essence was not yet.

Without the human essence, the Spirit of God could not be the flowing water of life. If God would be a flowing river of life, He must be constituted with the human nature of Jesus. For example, you cannot serve tea without water. In order to serve tea, you must add tea into the water. Before Jesus was resurrected, the Spirit of God was mighty, but He could not be the flowing life in man. If He would flow in man, He required the human nature of Jesus to be added into Him. If the Spirit of God were to be the flowing life in angels, He probably would not need the humanity of Jesus. But if He is to be the flowing life to man, He requires the human element. He needs the human nature of Jesus.

**CONFIRMATION BY
ANDREW MURRAY**

It was about eighteen or twenty years ago when we began to see this matter in John 7:37-39. At that time we began to minister these things according to what we had seen and experienced. I was always a little hesitant, however, to say that today the Spirit of Jesus contains not only the divine element but also the human essence. To say this is not a small thing. We realized that some might accuse us of teaching heresy when we said that the human essence is in the Holy Spirit. How could the Holy Spirit have any human element? However, according to the light we received from the Lord and the experiences we had had in the past, we saw that this is absolutely the truth. The Spirit of Jesus today contains the human element.

Then one day I was reading again chapter five of *The Spirit of Christ* by Andrew Murray. There I received the strongest confirmation. Chapter five has been in this book for years, but in the concept of many it is entirely new. Listen to what Andrew Murray says:

> We know how the Son, who had from eternity been with the Father, entered upon a new stage of existence when He became flesh. When He re-turned to Heaven, He was still the same only begotten Son of God, and yet not altogether the same. For He was now also, as Son of Man, the first-begotten from the dead, clothed with that glorified humanity which He had perfected and sanctified for Himself. And just so the Spirit of God as poured out at Pentecost was indeed some-thing new. When poured out at Pentecost, He came as the Spirit of the glorified Jesus, the Spirit of the incarnate, crucified, and exalted Christ, the bearer and communicator to us, not of the life of

God as such, but of that life as it had been interwoven into human nature in the person of Christ Jesus.

Christ came not only to deliver man from the law and its curse, but to bring human nature itself again into the fellowship of the Divine life, to make us partakers of the Divine nature. He could do this, not by an exercise of Divine Power on man, but only in the path of a free, moral, and most real human development. In His own person, having become flesh, He had to sanctify the flesh. Then from His nature, as it was glorified in the resurrection and ascension, His Spirit came forth as the Spirit of His human life, glorified into the union with the Divine, to make us partakers of all that He had personally wrought out and acquired, of Himself and His glorified life. In virtue of His atonement, man now had a right and title to the fulness of the Divine Spirit, and to His indwelling, as never before. And in virtue of His having perfected in Himself a new holy human nature on our behalf, He could now communicate what previously had no existence—a life at once human and Divine.

Christ had entered with our human nature, in our flesh, into the Holiest of all. There, in our place, and on our behalf, as man and the Head of man, He was admitted into the full glory of the Divine, and His human nature constituted the receptacle and the dispenser of the Divine Spirit. And the Holy Spirit could come down as the Spirit of the God-man—most really the Spirit of God, and yet as truly the spirit of man. He could come down as the Spirit of the glorified Jesus to be in each one who believes in Jesus, the Spirit of His personal life and His personal presence, and at the same time the Spirit of the personal life of the believer.

Just as in Jesus the perfect union of God and man had been effected and finally completed when He sat down upon the throne and He so entered on a new stage of existence, a glory hitherto unknown, so too, now, a new era has commenced in the life and work of the Spirit. He can now come down to witness of the perfect union of the Divine and the human, and in becoming our life, to make us partakers of it. There is now the Spirit of the glorified Jesus: He hath poured Him forth; we have received Him to stream into us, to stream through us, and to stream forth from us in rivers of blessing.

We must seek to know the New Life, the Life of Glory and Power Divine in human nature, of which the Spirit of the glorified Jesus is meant to be the Witness and the Bearer. We have the most intense personal interest in knowing and understanding what it means that Jesus is glorified, that human nature shares the life and glory of God, that the Spirit was not yet, as long as Jesus was not glorified. This is it of which Jesus says, never thirst, but shall have rivers of waters flowing out of him. This alone it is that satisfies the soul's thirst and makes it a fountain to quicken others; the Personal Indwelling of the Holy Spirit, revealing the Presence of the glorified Jesus.

FROM A LOWER
TO A HIGHER FORM

Stated in a simple and brief way, Jesus was God incarnated to be a man. Then He was crucified and resurrected. By crucifixion and resurrection, He was transfigured from a lower to a higher form. For example, suppose we have a seed with life in it. The form is low, but if the seed is sown in the earth, it grows, through decay and death, from a lower degree to a higher (see 1 Cor. 15:37, 42, 43). It was a seed, but now it has become a flower. The form of the seed is lower, while the stage of the flower is much higher. It was the same with Jesus when He was in the flesh before His crucifixion. His form was low, but by His crucifixion and resurrection, His form became higher, yet it still remained the same nature. The nature and essence was the same, but the form was different. He was flesh before His crucifixion, and He was still flesh after His crucifixion (Luke 24:39), but the form had changed. He did not through death and resurrection relinquish His flesh. He still retained the flesh, but in a higher, resurrected form. Then from this resurrected and ascended Jesus, the Spirit of Jesus came forth. Whatever is in Jesus, and whatever He has obtained and attained, are now all in this Spirit of Jesus.

Suppose we have a teapot full of tea from which we pour a cup of tea. Obviously, whatever is in the teapot will be exactly the same as what is in the cup. The tea in the cup is the same as that in the teapot. The Spirit of Jesus came forth from the very resurrected and ascended Jesus. By this we realize that today the Spirit of Jesus has not only the divine essence, but also the human essence of Jesus. There is not only divinity, but also humanity. We must consider who this "Me" is in Jesus' words: "If anyone thirst, let him come to Me and drink." It is not just the divine Person. It is a man. Hence, when we come to Jesus to drink of Him, we come to drink of this man. We drink not only of His divinity, but even the more of His humanity. Tea has an abundance of water in it; but we do not call it water, we call it tea.

THE NATURAL CONCEPT

I am afraid that many of us still think that whenever we come to Jesus to drink of Him, we drink of Him only as a divine Person. Few Christians today have the concept that when they drink of Jesus, they are not only drinking of a divine Person, but also of a human being. They are not drinking only of the divinity of Jesus, but even the more of His humanity.

I have seen many who have received the so-called Pentecostal experience with the manifestation of gifts. The strange thing was that in their daily life there was no flow of life. In the meetings, they spoke frequently in tongues and exercised many of the gifts, but when they were in their homes, the flowing of life was missing. For many years I have been observing this situation. Of course, concerning those who love the world and do not care for the Lord's interest, it is understandable that they do not have the flow of life. But what is the reason why those who are so much in the manifestation of the gifts do not have it? I believe the answer is in John 7. To have the flow of life, we all must drink of the humanity of Jesus. We must drink not only of the Spirit of God, but of the Spirit of an exalted Person, the Spirit of an exalted Man. Our understanding is that we drink only of the Spirit of God, but this is not adequate. If we drink only water, we are still short of tea. Today we need to drink some "tea." We need to drink of the humanity of Jesus. We need to drink of the resurrected and ascended man, Jesus. He is not only the Spirit of God, but also the Spirit of Jesus. The bountiful supply is not of the Spirit of God, but of the Spirit of Jesus Christ (Phil. 1:19).

NORMAL CHRISTIANS

Now let us apply all these things in a practical way. Many Christians would like to be angels. And we all expect to be powerful, spiritual, and heavenly. Perhaps you have never had the desire to be an angel, but you did hope to be a spiritual person full of power and able to do many miracles. But among millions of real Christians today, where is such a man? There are always many exaggerated reports, but once you go there, there is nothing. God's economy today is not like that. His purpose is that we drink of this uplifted humanity. God has no intention of making us angels, but of making us normal Christians with a normal humanity. Of course, we do not mean that we must be naturally human, but "Jesusly" human. We do not need any more of this poor, fallen humanity. Our humanity is not suitable to be brought to God the Father as the meal offering. Our humanity is only good for the lake of fire.

We must learn to take the humanity of Jesus to be a proper person. If under God's sovereignty you are a young man, you must behave yourself as a proper young man. I do not mean according to the worldly standard, but according to the humanity of Jesus. If under God's sovereignty you are a wife, a husband, a father, or a mother, you must be a proper one, not according to our standard, but according to God's standard. God's intention is that we would have a proper family life, not by our humanity, but by the humanity of Jesus. We should be different from all the other husbands or wives, whether they are good or bad. Their standard is not ours. Our standard is much higher and more practical than theirs. Ours is the humanity of Jesus.

Where is the humanity of Jesus today? We have already seen that the humanity of Jesus is in the Spirit of Jesus. If we will drink of the Spirit of Jesus, we will obtain the element of His humanity. As a husband, the Lord's humanity will strengthen you to be a husband who is absolutely agreeable with God's economy. It will not be according to any Christian standard or social standard. Neither Christianity nor society should be the standard of our human living. Our Christian living must be up to the standard of the humanity of Jesus.

Young people have asked me if Christians should have any kind of exercise for their health. We do need some exercise, but to exercise in the same way as the world is wrong. Even in the matter of bodily exercise, we need the humanity of Jesus. Some young people seeking to go on with the Lord have said that they could never exercise with unbelievers. I told them that they were one hundred percent right. I do not believe that any Christian who is one with the Lord can play in certain games and be on certain teams. Many times I partake of bodily exercise, but it is not according to my own natural humanity, but the humanity of Jesus. It is not a matter of whether we exercise or not. It is absolutely a matter of what kind of humanity we are exercising. If you exercise your own humanity, that is wrong. We all must be one with Jesus in whatever we do by taking Him as our humanity. If we cannot take His humanity in any course of action, we had better not do it. I do not mean we should not be a human being. We must be the best human being, but not by our own humanity. We need the humanity of Jesus, and this humanity is in the Spirit of Jesus.

THE FLOWING,
SATISFYING LIFE

It is in the humanity of Jesus that we have the life, the growth of life, and the flowing of life. It is this kind of flowing life that satisfies others. If we are drinking daily of the Spirit of Jesus, whatever we are will be a flow of life that will satisfy not only ourselves, but also others. Such a flow of life is not a matter of speaking in tongues or the manifestation of gifts; nor is it a matter of power, knowledge, or teaching; rather, it is a life that is always drinking of Jesus. This life is manifested not in a miraculous, divine, and heavenly way, but in a very human way.

To be a mother is a very human matter, but you should not be a mother by your own humanity, but by the humanity of Jesus. I do not mean that if formerly you did not properly care for your family as a mother, you must now be more human and care for your family in a better way. That is not the revelation from the Lord, but the culture of human society. What I mean is that, as a mother, you need to be a mother by the humanity of Jesus. As a wife, you need to be a wife by the humanity of Jesus.

We must be proper human beings, not by our humanity, but by the Lord's humanity. As a wife, we must be a wife by His humanity; as a husband, we must be a husband by

His humanity; as a student, we must be a student by the humanity of Jesus. Eventually we all will be so different, yet so human. We will be wives, husbands, students, parents, children, and teachers by the humanity of Jesus. If we are this kind of person, we will have the flow of life that will satisfy others. I believe that if all the brothers and sisters who are teachers would be this kind of person, there would be a real flow of life in the schools. The other teachers and students would realize that there is something satisfying, living, and flowing within you. They might not be able to explain it, but they would sense it.

If you are a brother who is drinking of Jesus by enjoying His humanity, it may seem that you do not have power, yet the flow of life within you will satisfy, convince, attract, and eventually convert others. This is the spreading of the gospel in the church life. This kind of gospel preaching does not depend so much on the power, but on the life that enjoys Christ's humanity.

The humanity of Jesus not only has much to do with the producing of gifted persons, but it also produces the flowing of the inner life to satisfy others. There is no other way to have such a flow of life but by enjoying the humanity of Jesus by drinking of the Spirit of Jesus all the time. We must have a real change in our concept. Whenever we pray, we must pray with this concept. Whenever we are drinking of the Spirit, we must drink of Him with this concept. We are not drinking of the Spirit for power, might, or miracles, but we are drinking of the Spirit of Jesus for the humanity of Jesus. As Andrew Murray said, it is not with the exercise of divine power, but with real human development. We need the proper humanity for our human life, and this proper humanity is not ours, but Jesus'. His humanity is not only the pure one, but also the resurrected, uplifted one. His humanity has been transfigured from a lower to a higher stage. And today we must drink of this uplifted, higher

humanity for our human life. May the Lord be gracious
to us that we may put all these things into practice.

CHAPTER THIRTEEN

THE HUMANITY OF JESUS
FOR THE SPIRITUAL WARFARE

Scripture Reading: Gen. 3:15; 1 John 4:2-3; Matt. 4:3-4; 8:29; 2 Cor. 10:1-4; 2 Tim. 1:7; 1 Thes. 4:3-4; 1 Cor. 6:15, 18-19

We have seen six main things in the past chapters on the meal offering: 1) it constitutes the proper worship to God; 2) it affords the proper diet for the priesthood; 3) it produces the standing boards; 4) it forms God's house by uniting the boards; 5) it produces the proper gifts; and 6) it produces the flow of life. Now in this chapter we must see that the humanity of Jesus is absolutely necessary for the spiritual warfare.

THE SEED OF A WOMAN

The spiritual warfare between the enemy and the saints is mainly dependent upon the humanity of Jesus. According to the Bible, the spiritual warfare is between Satan and God, yet God would never fight the battle by Himself. This is because Satan is a creature of God and a fallen creature at that. God is the Creator. The Creator would never fight with His creature; to do so would lower His position. This is why there is the need of man, and this is also why man was created by God. For the spiritual warfare, God needs another creature to deal with the fallen creature.

In Genesis 1, God says that He commits His dominion to man that man might subdue the earth. The word "subdue" includes the meaning of fighting. It is impossible to subdue something without a certain kind of fighting. God's intention was that man would war against Satan to subdue the rebellious earth. Yet we know how man was ruined by Satan. Satan knew that man was strategic in the spiritual warfare; therefore, he caused man to fall.

But, praise the Lord for Genesis 3:15! God promised that Christ would come as the seed of a woman. This seed of woman is a man, but a man who is different from the other man. The Bible says that Christ is the second man (1 Cor. 15:47). The first man failed, and then God sent the second man. Christ became a man to fight the battle for God. He partook of blood and flesh that through death He might destroy the Devil (Heb. 2:14). These verses reveal to us that Christ as a man fought with his humanity against Satan.

THE SON OF MAN

The temptation in the wilderness was the first confrontation between Satan and the Lord Jesus. There the Devil challenged the Lord by saying, "If you are the Son of God...." This was not only a challenge, but also a subtle attack. If the Lord Jesus had acknowledged at that time that He was the Son of God, He would have been defeated. But Jesus knew the subtle wiles of the enemy. Therefore, He answered, "Man shall not live by bread alone." He said, in other words, "Before you, Satan, I am not in the position of the Son of God, but in the position of man. I am not fighting against you as the Son of God, but as a man."

This is the reason why the demons cried out that Jesus was the Son of God when they met Him. They dared not confess that Jesus was the Son of Man. If they had, they would have been defeated. Nevertheless, the Lord silenced them. And this is why 1 John 4:2-3 says that every spirit that confesses not that Jesus Christ is come in the flesh is not the Spirit of God. This means that we all must confess that the Lord Jesus did come in the flesh. He came in the flesh not only to redeem us, but also to defeat Satan.

Christians today have the wrong concept. They believe that to fight the spiritual warfare we need spiritual power with something heavenly and divine. But listen to what Paul says in 2 Corinthians 10:1: "Now I Paul myself beseech you by the meekness and gentleness of Christ." Paul's beseeching was real fighting. The spiritual warfare between the enemy and the saints is not so much in divine power, but in the proper humanity. For the spiritual warfare, we need the humanity of Jesus. To fight the battle against the enemy, we must exercise the humanity of Jesus in our daily walk. Our family life needs the humanity of Jesus. Among the saints in the church we need the humanity of Jesus. In other words, if we are not proper in humanity, it is impossible for us to defeat Satan; we are defeated already. As long as we do not have the proper and normal humanity, we are already defeated.

SATAN'S TACTICS

Now I would like to speak more practically. And as I do, I look to the Lord for the covering of His prevailing blood as I expose the enemy's tactics. We are a tripartite being, with a spirit, a soul, and a body. Under the sovereignty of God, there is a boundary line drawn by Him to preserve the human spirit for His purpose. But Satan still can deaden the human spirit by means of the conscience. As long as our conscience is defiled, our spirit is deadened. If there is any defilement in our conscience, we can never be alive in the spirit. Hence, for the quickening of our spirit, we need a pure conscience. This is why we need the cleansing of the blood. The redeeming blood of Christ cleanses our conscience so that our spirit may be quickened.

God has drawn a boundary line to keep the human spirit for His purpose, but Satan has done and still is doing many things to damage both the soul and the body of man. All he can do to our spirit is to deaden it by means of the conscience. Praise the Lord that he can only do that much! However, according to the revelation of the Bible, Satan has liberty to do whatever he can to damage our mentality (the main part of the soul is the mind) and our body. This is the subtlety of the enemy.

We cannot tell how many mental cases there are in today's society; they are innumerable. This condition is not only a kind of mental illness, but it is also the subtle work of Satan. Experts will tell you that in the history of humanity, there have never been as many mental cases as today. According to our experience, it is easy to deal with demon possession, but it is really difficult for any Christian to deal with a mental case. Satan is so subtle today. He is doing whatever he can to damage the mentality of man.

<h3 style="text-align:center">SATAN'S TARGET</h3>

Satan's main target today is the young people. There are more mental cases among the young people than ever before. He does not care so much for the older generation, but he seeks to destroy the young people. Young people today have many kinds of concepts and movements. The source of all these concepts and movements is Satan. Satan has indoctrinated the mentality of the younger generation with all these things. We need to pray against this satanic tendency among today's young people. They do not know the risk they are running and the danger they are in. By considering how greatly they have changed from 1965 until today, we may realize how much the enemy is working. Satan is so subtle. He injects all his evil, satanic, devilish concepts and ideas into the young and fresh mentality of the young generation. This is his primary aim; he is out to damage the human mentality. This is why the Bible speaks so much of having a sound mind. Do you believe that the mentality of the younger generation today is sound? I would say that it is absolutely unhealthy. Their way of thinking is altogether dangerous. All the young brothers and sisters in the church life must be clear that the source of all this damage in the mentality is Satan. All the young people in the church must repudiate the concepts which they have held in the past. I do not care what kind of concept you had before you came into the church life; whatever you had, you must give it up. I am afraid that it may be something of Satan to damage your mentality.

The First Issue: Fornication

The issue of this kind of mental damage is of three categories. The first is fornication. In the past five or six years, I have heard much concerning this matter. Among today's young people, especially the so-called hippies, there are innumerable cases of fornication. They live just like animals. They do not even care for this word, "fornication." I believe that in their dictionary they do not have such a word. It is all done without shame. In the whole Bible, the greatest and most sinful act in God's eyes is idol worship. Fornication is second. Idol worship is an insult to God, and fornication is a damage to humanity. God created humanity for His divine purpose, but Satan damages this humanity by fornication.

On some occasions, the Lord Jesus tore down all of the rituals and ordinances of the Old Testament. But He did not tear down the law concerning fornication; rather He enforced it even the more. When the Pharisees spoke with Him about divorce, the Lord asserted that Moses had allowed them to divorce their wives because of the hardness of their hearts, but it was not so at the beginning (Matt. 19:3-9). The Lord enforced the commandment regarding fornication much more than it had been in the Old Testament times (Matt. 5:27-28). This is because nothing damages our humanity like fornication. Paul says that any act we commit is outside our body, but fornication damages our body (1 Cor. 6:18). Oh, the enemy is so subtle! He first injects so many devilish concepts into the mentality of the young people, and the first issue of this is fornication.

I would like to say a word to the young people. I am not speaking my own idea, but something from the divine Word. You young brothers and sisters should not enter into marriage so quickly, so lightly, and so easily. You must realize that marriage is a very holy relationship

(Heb. 13:4). No marriage should be broken (Matt. 19:6, 9). Anyone who breaks the marriage bond is exceedingly sinful to God. You must take the matter quite seriously to the Lord. Once you are married, you should never be divorced. Nothing offends the Lord so much as a wrong marriage, and nothing damages our humanity more than fornication. It is not just a moral matter; it is a matter of damaging the humanity which God created for His purpose.

I believe that many of you are acquainted with the cesspool of fornication existing among so many young people today. Three years ago when I was in San Francisco, I heard many detailed reports concerning this situation. I simply could not stand it. To me this is not human life, but animal life.

The Second Issue: Suicide

The second issue of the devilish concepts indoctrinated into young people's minds is to commit suicide. If you study the proper statistics, you will see that the number of suicides is much larger than it was five years ago. In the earlier years of my ministry I hardly ever heard someone tell me that he wanted to end his life. But in these last few years, a number of young believers have come to me and expressed such an intention. Where did this kind of thinking originate? Undoubtedly Satan has indoctrinated the mentality of the young people with this concept. We all must pray and stand against such subtlety of the enemy. Satan's whole purpose is to damage humanity so that man cannot be used for God's purpose.

The Third Issue: Mental Illness

The third issue of the indoctrination of devilish concepts is mental illness. If you will check with today's younger generation, you will see that so many do not have a strong mind. Their way of thinking and their concepts are altogether unsound and unhealthy. Paul says in 2 Timothy 1:7 that God has given us a spirit of a sound mind. We must be exceedingly healthy in our thinking, concepts, and ideas. We need to have a sound mind.

THE PROPER HUMANITY

Paul also says that every one of us should know how to possess his vessel in sanctification and honor (1 Thes. 4:4). We know that our "vessel" means our body. We all need to keep our body in sanctification and honor because our body is the temple of the Holy Spirit and a member of Christ (1 Cor. 6:15-16, 18-19). We should not misuse our body.

We must keep our mind healthy, and our body in sanctification. This means that we are in a battle. The church life is a real battle life. We are not battling with human beings, but against the subtle enemy, Satan. If we do not have a sound mind and if we do not keep our body in sanctification, we are defeated already. If we would fight the battle, we need a proper humanity. And a proper humanity is one not only with a strong, living spirit, but also one with a sound mind and a body kept in sanctification. This is the humanity which Satan fears so greatly. Consider today's society. Do you believe that you could find such human beings among the human race? I do not believe so. I even doubt if Christians in Christianity today have such a humanity. So many are dead in their spirit and unhealthy in their thinking, unsound in their mind. And, shameful as it is, even among Christians there is fornication. Satan seems to have gained the victory over all humanity.

But praise the Lord! The church is here with the humanity of Jesus. Such a humanity has a strong, living spirit, a clear, healthy, and sober mind, and a body kept in sanctification. This is the humanity that is qualified to fight the battle for God today. We long to see the church life in all the local churches with such a humanity. To some extent we can say that the church life is like this among us. But I feel burdened to share that the church life is not just a church life; it is also a battle life. We are not fighting against flesh and blood or any human beings, but against the principalities, the powers, and the darkness in the air.

If we do not have the proper humanity, we have lost the ground. Some may say that we have the ground of the precious blood. I agree; we do have the blood to cover us, but we still need the proper humanity with a living spirit, a sound and clear mentality, and a holy body, separated by God for His purpose. If we are wrong in any of these three matters, we are finished in the spiritual warfare. We simply do not have the ground to fight the battle.

Praise the Lord that the humanity of Jesus is not only necessary and sufficient to produce the standing boards, the uniting bars, the proper gifts, and the flow of life; it is even more necessary and sufficient for the spiritual warfare. For the church to fight the spiritual warfare, we all need the proper humanity. By ourselves we cannot be such a person, but He is such a Person in us, and His humanity is such a proper humanity for the spiritual warfare. The meal offering we present to God is composed of such a humanity. It is this humanity that constitutes the real worship to God, affords the priestly diet, produces the standing boards, forms God's building by the uniting bars, produces the proper gifts, gives us the flow of life, and fights the battle for us. We all must be bold in the humanity of Jesus so that we can fight the battle for God's kingdom.

CHAPTER FOURTEEN

THE HUMANITY OF JESUS FOR THE CHURCH SERVICE

Scripture Reading: 1 Tim. 2:8-10; 3:2-3, 8, 11, 14-15; 4:12; 5:1-2; 2 Tim. 4:22

THE DEFINITION OF SERVICE

In the local church the main feature is the service. But when we say "service," we do not mean a kind of Christian meeting. This is not our service. When we say "church service," we mean the practical serving in the church by many functions. For example, church service includes the functions of the elders, who care for many things in the responsibility of the church. The function of the deacons, who care for the church business and church affairs, is also included in the church service.

All those who know the Bible agree that the two books written by the Apostle Paul to Timothy cover this matter of the church service. These books help us to know the way to behave in the church, and this is quite practical. Paul says that he writes these things that we may know how to behave ourselves in the house of God, which is the church of the living God. Hence, the entire two books to Timothy are simply to reveal how we must practically behave ourselves in the church.

If we pray-read all the above verses which I have chosen from these two books, we will realize that they are all related to the matter of humanity. In Christianity today, most seeking ones pay their attention to the heavenly side. They say that we need power, the manifestation of the gifts, and the miraculous things. I recognize that

in the Lord's economy, there is a place for the miraculous.
I myself have experienced a good number of miraculous
things in my Christian life. But in these two books to
Timothy, which are written that the serving ones may
know how to behave themselves in the church, there is
nothing miraculous. Rather, these two books are very
much related to the proper humanity.

QUALIFICATIONS FOR ELDERS

In 1 Timothy 3, Paul gives us the qualifications of an
elder. He does not say that to be an adequate elder you
must have power, with all the gifts and miracles. No, in
his writings concerning the qualifications of an elder,
he does not even mention these things. Listen to what
he says: "The overseer then must be without reproach,
husband of one wife, temperate, of a sober mind, orderly, hospitable, apt to teach, not an excessive drinker,
not a striker, but forbearing, not contentious, not fond
of money" (1 Tim. 3:2-3). All these qualifications are
the virtues of humanity which are so necessary for
the eldership. Paul did not say a word about power and
gifts.

In the past years of my Christian life and work, I have
seen a good number of able persons with miraculous gifts
and power. But eventually what they were and what they
did became a distraction and damage to the building up
of the local church. In the long run, the local church can
only be built up by persons like those whom Paul has
described in this chapter. Through these persons, the
church will gradually be built up in a solid way. I believe
many of us have seen able persons who were powerful
and miraculous in gifts, yet eventually were of no benefit
for the building up of the church. They were capable
persons, yet they did not have the qualifications mentioned
by the Apostle Paul in 1 Timothy 3. They may build up
twelve inches by their spiritual capabilities, but eventually
they tear down fourteen inches by what they are. They
may build up something by what they do, but they tear
down more by what they are.

The building up of a local church requires the proper humanity. It does not depend on our work as much as it does on our humanity. To be temperate, sober, and forbearing is not a small thing. A local church does not need powerful elders, because sooner or later the church will be torn down by them. The church needs forbearing, gentle elders who do not give themselves to anything but the humanity of Jesus. I do not believe it is necessary to mention all these aspects. We all know what it means to be temperate, to exercise self-control, and to be forbearing, gentle, patient, and to make allowances for others. It takes the proper humanity to leave some margin for others. Out of this, there will be the real building up. We do need the proper humanity for the building up of a local church.

I am so happy for the last verse at the end of these two books: "The Lord be with your spirit. Grace be with you" (2 Tim. 4:22). If there were not such a verse, we would only have some good teachings; we could never fulfill them. Who can be such an elder? There is not one among us. Only the Lord Jesus Christ has such a humanity, and praise the Lord, He is in our spirit! We must learn to turn to our spirit to take the very humanity of Jesus. He is in our spirit, and where the Lord Jesus is, there is grace. Even He Himself is the grace. All we need for the building up of the church is the humanity of Jesus. We need all the virtues of His humanity. I cannot be such a person, but by enjoying His humanity in my spirit I can. It is not my duty; it is an enjoyment!

DEACONS AND DEACONESSES

There is also something concerning the deacons in these two books. First Timothy 3:8 says, "Deacons must similarly be grave, not double-tongued, not addicted to much wine, not seeking gain by base means." The first virtue that the deacons should have is to be grave. This means to be weighty and not so light. We all need to be grave in what we say and do. There must be some weight in everything we express. And we should not be double-tongued. This really calls for the humanity of Jesus.

Then Paul mentions something about the wives or deaconesses. "Women similarly must be grave, not slanderers, temperate, faithful in all things" (1 Tim. 3:11). Not only must the brothers who are the serving ones be grave, but also the sisters. They must be weighty and not slanderers. To slander is to say something in a light way. Our mouths should not be shut in the meetings; neither should they be too open in our talking. If we are too free in our talking, spontaneously we may slander or speak lightly of others. The Lord Jesus never slandered. He never spoke anything lightly. We do need the humanity of Jesus.

ALL BROTHERS AND SISTERS

Not only must the deacons and the deaconesses have these virtues, but so must all the brothers and sisters. Paul says, "I will therefore that men pray in every place, lifting up holy hands, without wrath and reasoning" (1 Tim. 2:8). Wherever we have wrath or reasoning, we are finished as far as prayer is concerned. When we turn away from wrath and give up all our reasoning, then we are ready to pray. But we cannot do this by ourselves. We need the Lord Jesus in our spirit to be our humanity. Then we will have the proper church service.

This brings us to 1 Timothy 2:9-10. These verses are for the sisters. "Similarly, that women adorn themselves in proper clothing with modesty and sobriety, not with braided hair and gold or pearls or costly clothing; but, what befits women professing godly reverence, by good works." The sisters must adorn themselves in proper clothing. The Greek word for proper means that which is arranged in a befitting way. Everything is very well arranged. Today we have two extremes. Some women need two or three hours to dress—that is one extreme. The other is that some do not care for their appearance at all. They dress in a sloppy way. The proper humanity is lacking in both extremes. Neither way of dress is arranged in a suitable way. For this reason Paul says that the women should adorn themselves in proper clothing with modesty.

The King James Version uses "shamefacedness" for "modesty." It really means to have a sense of shame. Sisters need to have such a sense. The women in the world have no sense of shame. According to God's creation and according to His natural law, women should have a sense of shame. God created them in this way. Satan's subtlety has encouraged women of today not to be shameful. The world says that it is a glory to be shameless. But a young lady without modesty and a sense of shame has lost all safeguard. A sense of shame is a kind of protection for the young ladies. Hence, Paul says that the sisters should adorn themselves with modesty or a sense of shame.

The way some women dress today is certainly not of a sober mind. Some young ladies wear their dresses too short, while others wear them too long. I do not believe that either way manifests sobriety. If the sisters take the humanity of Jesus, this humanity will give them a sober understanding in the way they should wear their clothing. There is not one verse telling us how long or how short our clothing should be, but there is this verse in 1 Timothy 2:9 telling the sisters to adorn themselves in proper clothing with modesty. I am not giving any regulations; I am just ministering something of the humanity of Jesus. If we really mean business to take Jesus as our humanity, He will tell us how we should dress.

At this point I would like to mention another verse in the Old Testament. Deuteronomy 22:5 says, "The woman shall not wear that which pertaineth unto a man, neither shall a man put on a woman's garment: for all that do so are an abomination unto the Lord thy God." Just last week while riding with a brother in his car, I was asked whether certain ones who were walking on the street were men or women. I answered that I simply did not know. I could not tell the difference. This is not a joke, this is a kind of abomination to the Lord. This kind of apparel leads to much fornication.

I say again that I am not giving any regulations for the church life. My burden is to minister the real, genuine, proper humanity of Jesus. I could never believe that the humanity of Jesus would allow any sister to adorn herself in a man's way, nor any brother to dress in a woman's way. The Lord says in His Word that this is an abomination to Him. It is not a small mistake or wrongdoing; it is an abomination to the Lord. We are fighting for the kingdom, and if we lose the ground, how can we fight the battle? The enemy will laugh at us. We will already be in his hands.

SOLID MATERIAL

We all need to be solid men and women with a proper humanity. In the New Jerusalem, there is not one piece of clay. All the materials are precious stones, very solid and strong. This is the humanity of Jesus. We all need to be very solid in the Lord's humanity. We should not remain as a piece of clay, but be transformed by the Lord's humanity into precious materials for God's building. The transforming element under the work of the Holy Spirit is the humanity of the Lord Jesus. If we are light and loose, without realizing the humanity of Jesus in our daily walk, there will be no standing of the church life and no spread of the Lord's testimony. For the standing of the Lord's kingdom and for the spreading of the local church, we all must be very solid. Then the church will be exceedingly strong to fight the battle.

The future of the Lord's recovery today does not depend so much upon the older brothers and sisters. It stands or falls with the young people. How much the church life will spread and be prevailing depends upon what kind of humanity the young people practice in the church life. If they will all take the humanity of Jesus, I can assure you that hall after hall will be added to the local church in Los Angeles. We will not only be a strong testimony to human society, but also a strong protest to the principalities and powers in the heavenly places. Furthermore, this may result not only in the spreading of the church life in Los Angeles, but this also might be the rescue of the U.S.A. In the past five or six years, Satan has sought to destroy this country because he knows the Lord needs it for His recovery. But I believe that the Lord in His sovereignty will preserve this country to recover and spread the church life all over the world.

A BEACHHEAD
ON THE EARTH

I have no intention to simply give some teachings concerning the five kinds of offerings in Leviticus. I have been speaking many messages on the humanity of Jesus because my burden is for the Lord's recovery. We must exercise the authority of the Lord to control the situation of the world. The world situation is not under the hand of the enemy, but under the hand of Christ. And we are His Body. We must claim and declare that Jesus Christ is the Lord of all the earth. The Lord needs cooperation. He needs a beachhead on the earth. He needs a place to put his feet. We must learn to cooperate with the Lord by taking His humanity. We should not be like so many defeated Christians who say that it is impossible to have the proper church life. This is a shame to the Lord and a glory to the enemy. We must tell the enemy that even before the Lord comes back, there will be something solid on this earth. We all need to pray, "O Lord, before You return, You must do something to put the enemy to shame—even here, in the city that is famous for Hollywood, the center of darkness. Praise You, Lord, that You are going to build up a strong church in this city that will really shame the enemy."

The young people in the church are extremely important today. How much they experience the humanity of Jesus means very much for the Lord's recovery. The church today does not need the teachings; the church is short of the real realization of the humanity of Jesus. So the young people must stand up by His grace to satisfy the Lord's requirements with His humanity. The devilish subtlety of the enemy is corrupting the young people today. Each of the young people in the church must be a different kind of person with a different kind of humanity. We must not care for the course of this age, but learn to experience the Lord as our proper humanity. This will build up something strong on the earth before the Lord comes.

CHAPTER FIFTEEN

THE HUMANITY OF JESUS
FOR OUR DAILY WALK

Scripture Reading: Titus 2:2-6; Gal. 5:22-23; Phil. 2:15; 4:8;
Matt. 5:13-16

We have seen that the humanity of Jesus is necessary
for the spiritual warfare and for the church service. If we
would fight the spiritual warfare for the kingdom of God,
we need a proper humanity. God needs man to deal with
His enemy, Satan, and this man is Jesus. Only one man
is qualified to fight the battle, and this man is our person.
Since He is our person within, His humanity is ours to
fight the battle for the kingdom of God.

Furthermore, to serve the Lord in the church in a
proper way, we need the humanity of Jesus. In his two
letters to Timothy, Paul covered three kinds of serving
ones. He first spoke of the elders, the overseers or bishops
(different titles for the same person). These are the leading
ones of the church. Then he referred to the deacons and
deaconesses, the brothers and sisters who are the serving
ones in the church. "Deacon" comes from a Greek word
which means one that serves. Paul also addressed the
Lord's servants, such as Timothy. Hence, there are three
kinds of serving ones in the church: the elders, the deacons
and deaconesses, and the workers for the Lord. All these
serving ones need the proper humanity. This is basic. Just
as the acacia wood was the standing element for the
boards of the tabernacle (Exo. 26:15), so the humanity of
Jesus is the standing element in all the spiritual things.

Whether we are in the spiritual warfare or in the church service, we need the proper humanity.

In this chapter we must see that the humanity of Jesus is also necessary for our daily walk. The humanity of Jesus is needed for fighting, for serving, and also for living. If we do not have the proper humanity, our daily walk cannot be proper.

THE EXPOSURE
OF OUR HUMANITY

Most of the older ones have already experienced the fact that the more we try to use our own humanity, the more we realize that it is absolutely disabled. Some of the younger ones may not yet believe that their humanity is so worthless. The older you are, however, the more you will recognize the depravity of your own humanity. Before we were sixteen years of age, we had a certain kind of confidence in our humanity. But once we were sixteen, we began to realize how hopeless we were. Then, after graduating from college, we realized that we were even more hopeless. And by the time we were married, we were fully convinced that our humanity was fallen beyond repair. Many young sisters, before they were married, thought that they were indeed wonderful, but marriage became a real exposure to them. After being married, although many would blame their husbands, they found out their true condition.

Now we are in the church, where there is no darkness. Everything is under the light, and everything is transparent. There is nothing that exposes us like the church. While we are in the church meetings, we are under the heavenly X-ray. Our humanity is exposed so that we may see the need of the proper humanity. Yet, when we are exposed by the heavenly light, we must immediately apply the blood. We need to pray, "O Lord, cleanse me from all of my past with Your blood. Cover me with Your blood."

UNDER THE BLOOD

Sometimes, however, we are quite foolish. Before we are enlightened in the church, we may not admit that we are wrong; we may not admit any kind of evil or corruption in ourselves. After we have become enlightened, however, we should never tell our failures to others. This is wrong. Rather, we must all apply the Lord's blood. All of the past is under the blood. We should never take anything out from under the blood to show others, especially in the meetings. This is absolutely unhealthy and unprofitable, and it is not according to the Scriptures. On one hand we need to be exposed by the divine light, but on the other hand, after being exposed, we have the covering of the redeeming blood. God has no intention to shame us by exposing us before others. He only wants us to see how worthless and hopeless we are in our humanity so that we may learn to take His humanity. After seeing this, we have the covering, cleansing blood. The exposing of the divine light is always followed by the cleansing and covering blood. We should not talk about ourselves and our past anymore. Once it has been exposed, it is under the covering of the blood. Let us forget about all of our failures in the past, for God's forgiving is His forgetting. Sometimes we try to remind God of the things that He has forgiven. But God simply does not have a memory for these things. Once He forgives, He forgets. Praise the Lord for His covering and cleansing blood!

THE PROPER HUMANITY
FOR ALL AGES

All of the above-mentioned verses concern our daily walk. Paul instructed Titus to help the saints in all age groups. "Aged men are to be temperate, grave, of a sober mind, healthy in faith, in love, in endurance; aged women likewise are to be in demeanor as befits the sacred, not slanderers, nor enslaved by much wine, teachers of what is good, that they may train the young women to be lovers of their husbands, lovers of their children, of a sober

mind, chaste, workers at home, good, subject to their own
husbands, that the word of God may not be blasphemed.
The younger men likewise exhort to be of a sober mind"
(Titus 2:2-6).

I am so happy that Paul mentioned aged men and aged
women, young men and young women. These are not the
elders or deacons, but the brothers and sisters in the
church. Without these verses, we might think that only
the elders and deacons must have the proper humanity,
and that it is not necessary for the others. But what Paul
told the elders he also said to the brothers and sisters. In
the last chapters, I stressed the fact that the young people
are the key persons for the Lord's recovery. But in this
chapter we see how the older ones must go before. Paul
does not charge the younger ones first, but the older ones.
They are the ones who must take the lead in the matter
of humanity.

We all know that the two books to Timothy and the
one to Titus were written in the latter time of Paul's
ministry. Therefore, by the time of these three writings,
Paul had more experience. What he wrote in these three
books, therefore, was based more upon his experience.
These books are quite different from Romans, 1 Corinthians, Galatians, and other books which were written in
his earlier ministry. For example, in 1 Corinthians 7, Paul
told the believers that it is better not to be married,
especially for the sisters. But when he wrote 1 Timothy 5,
his attitude had changed. In Timothy he said that all the
young widows should be married. Why is this? Because
after many years, Paul had more experience. In these
three books he does not say much concerning doctrines.
In these later books he simply stresses the proper
humanity. In his other letters he never stressed the matter
of humanity as much as he did in these three. If we would
read 1 and 2 Timothy and Titus again with this attitude,
we would see that the central and basic point of which
Paul speaks is the matter of humanity. This is because
he had learned from experience, that for the long run, the

church life requires the proper humanity much more than other things.

When Paul wrote these three books, the church was degraded, and under that kind of degradation, the need was not mainly for teachings or gifts, but human virtues. I believe that the message of these three books just fits today's situation. We are under such a degradation. What is the proper cure for this age? What is the proper dose for this generation? The answer is the proper humanity that comes from the man Jesus. The proper humanity is the only healing power for today's generation. I have confidence that the Lord will use the church as a remedy for today's crooked and perverse generation. The remedy for such a generation is a church with the proper humanity. I have the full assurance that if the young people in the church take the humanity of Jesus, they will be the proper remedy for this generation.

It is not just a matter of shouting, "Hallelujah, Jesus is Lord!" We need the humanity of Jesus to back up our shouting. Then there will be the manifestation of the humanity of Jesus in the schools, on the jobs, and wherever the brothers and sisters are. There will be the shining of the humanity of Jesus into the darkness of this generation.

Paul mentions something concerning the matter of humanity in these three books, and he also speaks of human virtues in Philippians 4:8. "For the rest, brothers, whatever is true, whatever is honorable, whatever is pure, whatever is lovely, whatever is well-spoken of, if there is any virtue and if any praise, take account of these things." It is clear that these are all human virtues. He also tells us in this book that we are the children of God as lights shining in this world among a crooked and perverted generation (2:15).

THE FRUIT OF THE SPIRIT

In Galatians 5:22-23, Paul speaks of the fruit of the Spirit. The Spirit here refers to the Spirit of the humanity of Jesus. Paul does not speak of the fruit of the Spirit of God or the fruit of the Holy Spirit. This is the Spirit of Jesus, because all of the items mentioned are human virtues. "But the fruit of the Spirit is love, joy, peace, longsuffering, kindness, goodness, faithfulness, meekness, self-control; against such things there is no law." The things that are mentioned in these verses are not divinely powerful or miraculous. They are something of humanity—but not of our humanity. These things come forth only from the humanity of Jesus.

Suppose we have two brothers before us. One has a marvelous healing gift, and the other takes the humanity of Jesus to be gentle, meek, joyous, and full of self-control and longsuffering. Which of these two brothers would you prefer? I am afraid that many Christians would pay little attention to the one with the proper humanity. All would admire the one with the healing gift, and he would even be advertised in the newspaper. I have never seen an advertisement in the newspaper concerning a Christian who is exercising the proper humanity.

Paul did not say that the fruit of the Spirit is divine healing. Healing is something which is performed outwardly, but gentleness, meekness, and self-control are part of one's being. Our being is much more important than our doing. Hudson Taylor, the founder of the China Inland Mission, once said that God pays more attention to what we are than what we do. Many Christians pay too much attention to what people do, rather than what they are.

I do believe that today in the church life the Lord is going to recover His humanity. We not only need His power; we need His humanity. We not only need what He can do; we need what He is. I cannot believe that the miraculous gifts are the remedy for today's generation. Rather, the proper humanity shining forth through the young brothers and sisters will be a strong testimony and remedy to this present age. And this humanity will also cause us to have the strongest church life. The fruit of the Spirit is just the expression of the humanity of Jesus.

THE SALT OF THE EARTH
AND THE LIGHT OF THE WORLD

The Lord Jesus told us in Matthew 5 that we are the salt of the earth and the light of the world. The function of salt is to kill corrupting elements so that things may be preserved. There is much corruption on the earth today. Everywhere you go you can see the germs of corruption. How we need the salt! And the basic element of the salt is nothing but the humanity of Jesus. The humanity of Jesus in our daily walk is the heavenly salt. The more we live by the humanity of Jesus, the more salty we will be. With this humanity, there is the killing power for all the corrupting germs. The more we apply, experience, and live by the humanity of Jesus, the more we will be the salt to this corrupted and corrupting generation. Hence, we see what a responsibility we have. It is not just a matter of shouting, "Jesus is Lord!" but of being the salt with the salting power. We all need the real transformation that comes from the application of the humanity of Jesus in our daily walk.

Furthermore, the problem today is not only a matter of corruption, but also of darkness. How dark it is today! I simply do not dare to read the papers. The whole situation is under darkness. But, hallelujah, the church is the lampstand, and we are the light! Yet we can be the light only by taking the humanity of Jesus.

Now the importance of the meal offering in Leviticus is apparent. When we come to the last three offerings, we will see that they are based upon the first two. The burnt offering and the meal offering are the basic offerings, and all the other offerings are built upon them. But the meal offering is more weighty and even more basic than the burnt offering.

In all spiritual matters the basic structure is the

humanity of Jesus. We have already seen nine or ten matters which are produced by the Lord's humanity. If the tabernacle had not had the standing boards, it would have been in confusion. The basic structure of all spiritual things is the humanity of Jesus. This humanity is the heavenly salt and the divine light. Without this humanity, the salt loses its flavor. May the Lord be merciful to us that His humanity may be wrought into our Christian walk and daily living.

Chapter Sixteen

THE HUMANITY OF JESUS
FOR THE LORD'S RECOVERY

Scripture Reading: 2 Tim. 3:1-5, 16-17; 2:21-22; 1:7; 4:22

The eleventh point concerning the humanity of Jesus is that it is necessary for the Lord's recovery. We must realize that the letters written by Paul to Timothy and Titus were written for recovery, because at that time degradation had already occurred in the church life. History tells us that the Roman Empire began to decline at exactly the same time as the church, during the last part of the first century. By reading 2 Timothy 3, we see the situation that existed at the end of the first century. Paul said that in the last days perilous times would come, and it was not long before this prophecy was fulfilled. History tells us that by the end of the first century, there was much corruption and ruin in the society of the Roman Empire.

TODAY'S SITUATION

We are in exactly the same kind of situation today as was the early church. At that time the church was degraded and society was ruined, and it is clear that it is the same today. Therefore, we must all realize that we are in a situation that requires the Lord's humanity for His recovery. There must be a group of people to stand against the tide of this age. But what is the way for us to stand? Is it by divine power? It is rather difficult to find much in these three books about divine power. These books are from Paul's later ministry which has very much to do with the humanity of Jesus.

We have previously mentioned from these books that the humanity of Jesus is necessary for the church service, which involves the co-workers, elders, deacons, and deaconesses. All the verses related to these serving ones mention something concerning the human virtues of the proper humanity. Paul did not tell Timothy to be an example in power, but in love, in word, and in the way he conducted himself. This is all a matter of humanity. All the qualifications for the church service are human virtues. The same principle applies to the Christian walk. To deal with the older brothers and sisters as well as the young brothers and sisters requires the uplifted humanity of Jesus.

It is abundantly clear from these three books that we need a strong, adequate, and proper humanity in order to have the Lord's recovery in such a degraded time. We do not need divine power as much as we need the humanity of Jesus to stand up in such a degraded age. This is the standing power of the acacia wood. If we follow the course of today's age, we are like the jellyfish, without any backbone. Whatever way the tide goes, the jellyfish follow. We do need a strong backbone to stand against the current of today's age for the Lord's recovery, and this backbone can issue only from the humanity of Jesus. The background of these three books (the degradation of the church and the corruption of society) is exactly like today's situation. Therefore, these three books should really be applied to us today.

TWENTY-ONE ITEMS

The first five verses of 2 Timothy 3 show us the situation that existed at that time: "But know this, that in the last days difficult times shall come; for men shall be lovers of self, lovers of money, boasters, arrogant, revilers, disobedient to parents, unthankful, unholy, without natural affection, implacable, slanderers, without self-control, savage, nonlovers of good, traitors, reckless, blinded with pride, lovers of pleasure rather than lovers of God; having a form of godliness, but having denied its power; from these also turn away."

In these verses there are exactly twenty-one items. The first is lovers of self. I believe that we all know that humanity is a matter of love. Human beings are not machines; they are loving beings. If there is no love, humanity will vanish. Suppose all the members of a family have no love. What kind of family will that be? Therefore, the first aspect of humanity is love. But love must be used in the proper way. If it is used wrongly, it is exceedingly dangerous. But the proper use of love requires the proper humanity. Therefore, the first cause of corruption of society is the misuse of love. Paul tells us that men will become lovers of self.

The second item is lovers of money. I do not believe that money has ever been more lovable than at the present time. The third is boasters. How the young people are boasting today! The fourth is arrogance. They are not only proud, but arrogant. The fifth is revilers. We see so much of this today. The sixth is disobedient to parents. This is very prevalent today. It seems that human ethics have been changed. Some even say that it is good to be disobedient to parents. This comes straight from the Devil. Any disobedience comes from Satan, the rebellious one. He is the source of all rebellion.

The seventh item is unthankfulness. The mood today is to be ungrateful to parents, ungrateful to grandparents, ungrateful to brothers and sisters, and even ungrateful to country. This is the real picture of today's generation. And today's younger generation is simply reaping the things sown by the older generation. The eighth is unholiness. People today simply hate to be holy. The ninth is to be without natural affection. Too many people do not have natural affection today, and they even boast of it.

The tenth item is implacable. This means that these people do not like to make peace with others. They do not like to forgive others, and they do not like to be reconciled to others. The more trouble they can make, the better. The more riots, the more turmoil, the happier they are. This is a prophecy which was fulfilled at the end of the first century and will also be fulfilled at the end of this age. In the prophecies of the Bible, there is always a double fulfillment: one at the present time, and the other in the future. I do believe that what we are seeing today is part of the fulfillment. People simply do not like to make peace. They talk about peace, yet they act the contrary.

The eleventh item refers to slanderers. These people always criticize good reports and carry evil reports about others. They are continually making all kinds of false reports. The twelfth item is without self-control. So many today have cast off all restraint. The thirteenth is savage men. They are like wild beasts—not only fierce but also wild. The fourteenth is nonlovers of good. In today's world situation, evil and devilish people are teaching others to hate all good things. Instead of lovers of good, they are nonlovers of good. The fifteenth is traitors. These are those who are always betraying others. The sixteenth is those who are reckless. The seventeenth is those who are blinded with pride. The eighteenth is lovers of pleasure, and the nineteenth is nonlovers of God.

The last two items are seen in the phrase, "having a form of godliness, but having denied its power." The twentieth is the form of godliness. This may refer to those who go to church on Sunday. You may say that they have a form of godliness, but they deny the power, which is the twenty-first item. What is the power of godliness? It is Jesus Christ. Too many Christians have a form of godliness, but they care nothing for Christ. They have the religious form, but they do not have Christ.

Nearly all of these twenty-one items are related to human virtues. We must love in a proper way. We must be right with God, we must be right with our parents, and we must be right with others. We must even be right with ourselves. Too many today are not right with themselves. They are wrong with God, wrong with their parents, wrong with each other, and even wrong with themselves. In a sense, they are not human. They are out of the proper humanity. Their humanity has been ruined to the uttermost.

A RECOVERY WORK

The Lord is doing a recovery work in which He needs a people who realize and take Him as their humanity. In the midst of the degradation of the churches and the corruption of society, we are here for the Lord's recovery. But for this we need a strong and proper humanity. It is not sufficient simply to shout, "Hallelujah!" or "Jesus is Lord!" It is not enough to have divine healing or the so-called power from on high. We must show this generation, and even the entire universe with the Devil and all his demons, that we are taking the proper humanity to fulfill God's purpose. We must declare and even proclaim to this universe that we are here as genuine men. We are here as a corporate man taking Jesus as our humanity. This will terrify the enemy. The tempter came to the Lord Jesus and said, "If You are the Son of God...." But the Lord Jesus answered by referring to Himself as a man (Matt. 4:3-4). That terrified the enemy. We must be "Jesusly" human. Every member of the church in the Lord's recovery must be a proper man, even an "acacia" man. This will be a strong testimony, and the mouth of the enemy will be shut.

I realize that many people today are waiting to criticize the local churches. Whenever they are wrong, they will justify it, but when we are wrong in anything, they will tell everyone. There is only one way to shut their mouths, and that is by expressing the humanity of Jesus. Their conscience will have to agree with the proper humanity. So many opposing ones are waiting for the churches to fail. They are looking for any failure on our part. It is really a kind of suffering to us. Many of us were never opposed or criticized so much as when we came into the local church. To be in the local church is to collect much criticism from Christianity. But this is not really criticism, it is something of the battlefield. But we cannot fight the battle without the proper humanity of the Lord Jesus. The proper humanity for the Lord's recovery will surely shut all the critical, opposing mouths.

THE PROPER WAY

Then what is the way to enjoy such a humanity? In the above verses we are able to see five main items. By these we can see the Apostle Paul's concept concerning the way to take the humanity of Jesus. The first was to call on the name of the Lord from a pure heart. "Flee youthful lusts, and pursue righteousness, faith, love, peace with those who call on the Lord out of a pure heart" (2 Tim. 2:22). When we call on the name of the Lord, we are really taking His humanity into us. Then Paul referred to the Scriptures: "All Scripture is God-breathed..." (2 Tim. 3:16). All Scripture is breathed out by God to make us genuine and proper men of God. We not only need to call on the Lord, but we must also breathe in every word of the Scriptures. This is simply to pray-read the Word. How important are these two items for taking the Lord's humanity! We must call on the Lord, and we must breathe in His Word.

The third item is the Body life. Paul did not say simply to call on the Lord by yourself, but with "those" (2 Tim. 2:22). This is a corporate life. We enjoy the Lord's humanity by being with those who call on the Lord out of a pure heart. Fourth, Paul tells us that we have a spirit to exercise. "For God has not given us a spirit of cowardice, but of power and of love and of a sober mind" (2 Tim. 1:7). And fifth, we have a wonderful Person in our spirit: "The Lord be with your spirit" (2 Tim. 4:22).

We have these five matters to practice: calling on the Lord, breathing in the Scriptures, having the Body life, exercising our spirit, and realizing the Lord Jesus within our spirit. This reveals the concept of the Apostle Paul.

How can we enjoy the humanity of Jesus? Simply by these five things. We have to call on the Lord, we must breathe in the Word, and we must do these things in a Body way in the church life. For this we have such a strengthening factor in our spirit. The Lord Jesus, who is the real humanity, is in our spirit. By exercising our spirit to call on Him and to breathe in the Word in a corporate way, we simply enjoy His humanity.

Suppose that I am a young man, seventeen years of age. If I exercise my spirit to call on the Lord and to pray-read His Word with the brothers and sisters, do you believe that I could be disobedient to my parents? I do not believe so. There would be no need of anyone telling me to obey my parents. Spontaneously, I would be obedient to my parents because of the humanity of Jesus within me. And if I have been doing these things in the church life, do you believe that I could be boastful or arrogant? Never! Since I would have the proper humanity within me, I could never behave in that way. This issue does not come by teaching, but by feeding on the Lord Jesus. The proper enjoyment of the humanity of Jesus will swallow up all the negative things and replace them with all the positive things.

We must pray for the entire situation of the Lord's recovery, that all the brothers and sisters in the local churches may have a full enjoyment of the humanity of Jesus. Then we will be the acacia boards, standing steadfastly against the current of this evil age. This will be our strong testimony, and this will bring the recovery of the local church life to all the leading cities.

CHAPTER SEVENTEEN

THE HUMANITY OF JESUS FOR GOD'S KINGDOM

Scripture Reading: Gen. 1:26, 28; Ezek. 1:26; Dan. 7:13-14; Matt. 19:28; John 5:27; Rom. 14:17; 1 Cor. 6:9-10; Gal. 5:19-21; Eph. 5:3-5; Rev. 20:4

IMAGE AND DOMINION

In this last chapter on the meal offering we will see how the humanity of Jesus is necessary for the kingdom. In the above verses, we can see from Genesis 1 to the end of Revelation that humanity has much to do with God's kingdom. In the beginning, God created man not only to be in His image, but also to have dominion. "And God said, Let us make man in our image, after our likeness: and let them have dominion over the fish of the sea, and over the fowl of the air, and over the cattle, and over all the earth, and over every creeping thing that creepeth upon the earth....And God blessed them, and God said unto them, Be fruitful, and multiply, and replenish the earth, and conquer it: and have dominion over the fish of the sea, and over the fowl of the air, and over every living thing that moveth upon the earth" (Gen. 1:26, 28 lit.).

Image is a matter of expression. God created man in His own image that man may express God. The image of God is for the expression of God. But man was also created to exercise dominion over all the earth. This is the kingdom. The word "over" is used five times in Genesis 1:26—one time for the living things in the air, and three times for the living things on the earth. And it is especially mentioned that man is to have dominion over the creeping things. Satan, who is called the old serpent, is the head of all the creeping things; therefore, this means that man must have dominion over Satan, the rebellious one. God's intention is for man to control the earth.

Then in Genesis 1:28, the Lord says that man must subdue or conquer the earth. If there were nothing rebellious on the earth, there would be nothing to subdue. But because of the rebellion of Satan, there is the need of subduing the earth. God would never do it Himself, although He could. To deal with a rebellious creature would lower His position as Creator. Therefore, God needs another creature, a man, to subdue the rebellious creature. This is a matter of God's kingdom.

THE KINGDOM, THE POWER, AND THE GLORY

At the end of the Lord's prayer, we have the words, "Yours is the kingdom, and the power, and the glory forever." Here we see the kingdom, the power, and the glory. Without the kingdom, it is impossible to exercise power, and without power there is no glory. Glory depends upon power, and the power is exercised only in the kingdom. Hence, God needs a kingdom on the earth so that He may exercise His power to manifest His glory. God's intention is to build a kingdom on the earth, and in this kingdom God will be free to exercise His authority and power. It is in this realm of His authority in the kingdom that God can express His glory. Glory is simply the manifestation of God Himself. When God is manifested, that is glory.

For example, the glory of an electric light is just the manifestation of the invisible electricity. The glory and the light of electricity is the electricity itself manifested. When electricity is manifested, the glory in the light appears. God is a mystery; He is hidden and invisible. Like the mystery of electricity, we can see the light when the electricity is manifested. Likewise, when God is manifested, we can see His glory. However, to express

God's glory, a realm is needed where God may exercise His authority and power. This realm of authority and power is God's kingdom.

In a sense, the church on earth today is God's kingdom. This is shown in Romans 14:17: "For the kingdom of God is not meat and drink; but righteousness, and peace, and joy in the Holy Spirit" (lit.). Romans 12 speaks of the Body, the church. Then in chapter fourteen Paul speaks of the church, not as the Body, but as the kingdom of God. If we put these chapters together, we can see that the kingdom of God mentioned in Romans 14 is just the church. The church is not only the house of God or the Body of Christ, but also the kingdom of God. And in the kingdom of God, the main factors are God's authority, God's reigning, and God's ruling. God's kingdom does not require angels; God's kingdom needs man. The need is for humanity.

<h2 align="center">A MAN ON THE THRONE</h2>

Let us look at Ezekiel 1:26: "And above the firmament that was over their heads was the likeness of a throne, as the appearance of a sapphire stone: and upon the likeness of the throne was the likeness as the appearance of a man above upon it." Ezekiel saw a vision of a throne in the clear sky. And on the throne there was one sitting like the son of man. We would think that God would be sitting on the throne, but Ezekiel saw a man! In this book Ezekiel was called the son of man ninety-three times by the Lord. The whole concept of this book in God's divine vision is altogether focused on the matter of man. God needs a man. Our concept is that the one on the throne of the whole universe is God, but here is a verse telling us that the one who is sitting on the throne is a man.

Humanly speaking, it is easy for God to establish a kingdom by Himself. But Satan would only belittle this. We can see the belittling of Satan in the book of Job. Satan told God that Job feared Him simply because He blessed him, and if God were to take away all the blessings, Job would not fear Him. Satan thought that God bought Job by His blessings. But what a glory to God that Job still feared him when all the blessings were taken away! That was a real shame to Satan. When God stripped Job of so many things, he still loved God. He loved God not for the blessings, but for God himself.

God would never establish a kingdom by Himself. He knows what Satan would say if He did. Therefore, God created man, and then left this man in a garden without any fence. God did this purposely so that Satan could try whatever means he chose to attempt to frustrate God's plan. But after Satan damaged man, God's wisdom was even further expressed. God had created a good and perfect man, yet Satan damaged him and made him a rebel and a sinner. But God would regenerate this man and make a new man. Out of all Satan's destruction, God would build something new. And praise the Lord, God did it!

A NEW HUMANITY

Before we were saved we were just a sketch of destruction. But out of this sketch of destruction God has regenerated us to become a new humanity. This is a glory to God and a shame to Satan. As long as the church has the proper humanity, God can tell Satan, "Even in Los Angeles, the movie capital of the world, I have built up a humanity against you. I have not done it by angels or by Myself, but with the human beings you damaged. I have built up a new humanity." What a glory to God to be able to say this to Satan! Even Satan will realize that the more he damages man, the more glory God will get.

My burden is that the veil may be taken away so that we will all know God's ultimate intention. His purpose is not merely that we may all go to heaven. God's ultimate intention is to build up a kingdom with His humanity on this earth. Do not think that I was a good person before I was saved. I certainly was not. But I am here ministering something of Christ to all of you. This is a glory to the Lord and a shame to Satan. All Satan can say is that the little man whom he once damaged is now ministering Christ.

The principle applies to all of us. Some of the young people in the church were hippies in the past. Only the Lord knows the kind of life they lived. For all of these so-called "ex-hippies" to take the Lord's humanity for a proper human life is the biggest shame to Satan. Satan would have to say, "Five years ago I greatly damaged these young people, yet today they have such a proper humanity. I have no face to stay in Los Angeles." This is for the kingdom of God.

A BALANCED HUMANITY

Look at the corruption and lawlessness of today's situation, especially among the young generation. The young people long to be liberated and free in everything. They want to be liberated from the yoke of their parents, from the yoke of their schools, from the yoke of the police, from the yoke of the neighborhood, and even from the yoke of the constitution of the country. Their concept is that the more wild they are, the more free they are. They do not want to be bound in any way. But have you realized that this kind of concept comes from Satan, the source of lawlessness? He is the source of all the rebellion against authority, because he hates the kingdom of God.

For God to have a kingdom on the earth among the younger generation, there is the need of a group of people to be redeemed and regenerated in order to take the humanity of Jesus. By this humanity they are balanced in all things. For example, not long ago the neckties were quite narrow. But today, they are wider than ever. They look like a big fan. Don't you think that is rather extreme? Of course, outward adjustment will never work, but if we take the humanity of Jesus, I do believe that we will not be that extreme. By taking the Lord's humanity, we will never be out of balance. We must be under God's heavenly ruling. If we are, even our neckties will manifest our balance. Our shoes and our clothing will give others the impression that we are absolutely sane, healthy, and sober. We are sober and balanced. Everything is properly proportioned. We know what kind of shoes we must wear; we even know how much we can spend to buy a pair of shoes. We are so balanced, so moderate, so sober, and so healthy. We must be able to make such a declaration to the whole universe. All the demons know the true situation much better than we do. If we make such a declaration, they may point to our hair. Our hair may indicate that we are not so sound. They may point out the pair of shoes that we bought last week. We may say that we are balanced, but actually we may not be. We may be simply following the modern ways of today's evil generation. When they wear strange things, we follow and wear them too. Only unbalanced people do this. This is why there are many mental cases. However, we are under the covering of the Lord's prevailing blood. By His victorious grace we can boldly declare to Satan that we are not mental cases. We are moderate in everything. But it is not because of us; it is by the humanity of Jesus. We enjoy His humanity in our daily walk.

A MAN TO JUDGE

The Son of Man is sitting on the throne not only in Ezekiel, but also in Daniel 7:13-14: "I saw in the night visions, and, behold, one like the Son of man came with the clouds of heaven, and came to the Ancient of days, and they brought him near before him. And there was given him dominion, and glory, and a kingdom, that all people, nations, and languages, should serve him: his dominion is an everlasting dominion, which shall not pass away, and his kingdom that which shall not be destroyed." Daniel saw this vision of the Son of Man coming to the Ancient of days to receive the kingdom. We know that this is the Lord Jesus. The Lord Jesus Himself told us of the time when the Son of Man will sit on the throne

(Matt. 19:28), and John 5:27 tells us that God gave Him the authority to execute judgment because He is the Son of Man. As a man, He is qualified to execute God's judgment.

HUMAN VIRTUES FOR THE KINGDOM

First Corinthians 6:9-10, Galatians 5:19-21, and Ephesians 5:3-5 are verses which show us the humanity which is not fit for God's kingdom. I do not even like to mention all these things; they are the negative side of human virtues. These verses mean that if we do not have the proper human virtues, we are finished as far as the kingdom of God is concerned. If we mean business with God to participate in His kingdom, we must have the proper human virtues. It is impossible to have these virtues by ourselves. But thank God that we have One who is the proper, unique Man dwelling in our spirit. Such a One with all His proper human virtues is in us to be our humanity. Paul says in Ephesians 5 that we should not allow these negative things to be even named among us as is fitting for saints (Eph. 5:3). We must realize that as saints, we are holy human beings. Therefore, our mouths should never be used even once to mention anything filthy. We do need such a human virtue. We should never mention our sordid failures in the past. God has forgotten them, so let us forget them. We never need to speak of things like that. Rather we should say, "Praise the Lord!" and give thanks to God.

All these virtues show us that for the kingdom of God we need the proper human virtues, and for all these proper human virtues, we need the humanity of Jesus. When we have this humanity we will not only be in the kingdom of God, we will be the kingdom of God. The church in Los Angeles is the kingdom of God in Los Angeles. Satan has been deceiving the church for many generations. Either he keeps Christians from spiritual things, or he causes them to pay their attention to spiritual things on the divine side, neglecting their proper humanity. But the Lord is going to recover the humanity of Jesus. This is another item which the Lord has recovered in order to strengthen His recovery of the church life. Without the proper humanity, it is impossible to have a proper local church life.

In all the local churches, people must see the glory of God expressed in human beings. How they behave, how they dress, how they contact one another, how they behave in their family life, and how they act in their daily walk must be really human, yet manifest the glory of God. This is the proper church life.

Finally, when we come to the end of the Bible, we see the overcomers who will reign with Christ a thousand years. "And I saw thrones, and they sat upon them, and judgment was given to them. And I saw the souls of those who had been beheaded because of the testimony of Jesus and because of the word of God, and who did not worship the beast nor his image, and did not receive the mark on their forehead and in their hand; and they lived and reigned with Christ a thousand years" (Rev. 20:4). How do all of these overcomers become qualified to reign with Christ? I do believe that it is by the humanity of Jesus being worked into them.

May the Lord help us to realize how much we need His humanity. We need all the human virtues in order to put Satan to shame. Every bit of our daily walk must conform with the Lord's humanity in our spirit. If the Lord's humanity does not agree with what we are doing, we must say, "Lord, I will never go against Your humanity within me in this matter. I will simply give it up." If we do this, we will all have a proper daily life in the humanity of Jesus. Then we will have a proper church life, and this church life will be God's kingdom on the earth today. This will be a real shame to Satan and a real boast to God.

CHAPTER EIGHTEEN

THE EXPERIENCE OF CHRIST
AS OUR PEACE OFFERING

Scripture Reading: Lev. 3:1-17; 7:11-21, 29-34; Num. 10:10; Deut. 27:7; Col. 1:20-22a; Rom. 5:1; Luke 15:23

The past fourteen chapters have been on the meal offering, and I do believe that by them the Lord has shown us something of the humanity of Jesus. Now we come to the peace offering. From the above verses, it is clear that the presenter has to lay his hands upon the peace offering. "And if his present be a sacrifice of peace offering, if he present it of the herd, whether it be a male or female, he shall present it without blemish before the Lord. And he shall lay his hand upon the head of his offering, and kill it at the door of the tent of meeting: and Aaron's sons the priests shall sprinkle the blood upon the altar round about" (Lev. 3:1-2, lit.). To lay your hands upon the offering means that you identify yourself with what you offer. This means that you are declaring your oneness with the offering which you are presenting to God. And this present which you offer is the Lord Jesus Christ.

ONE IN REALITY

How can we be one with the Lord? Is this just a positional matter, or is it possible to be one with Him in reality? If so, how can we be one with Him? How can we lay our hands on Christ as a present to God? The way is to exercise our spirit. To lay our hands on the offering, which is Christ, is a picture. And to exercise our spirit is the fulfillment today. To exercise our spirit really makes us one with Christ. When we come to present Christ to God as the peace offering, we need to exercise our spirit to declare that we are one with Christ. Thus, it is not just a positional matter; it is also a practical matter. We are practically one with Christ in our spirit. "He that is joined to the Lord is one spirit" (1 Cor. 6:17). Hence, when we come to the tent of meeting to present Christ to God as a kind of present, we need to exercise our spirit that we might be one with Him. This is the first point concerning the peace offering.

ONLY IN THE TENT OF MEETING

The second point is that the peace offering can be presented and enjoyed only in the tent of meeting. It is not to be enjoyed at home, but it must be brought to the door of the tent of meeting. We know that today the tent of meeting is the meetings of the local church. It is rather difficult for any one of us to enjoy Christ as the peace offering in our own home. We must be in the church meeting in order to have the position to enjoy Christ as the peace offering.

Of course, I realize that some will say that the Lord is omnipresent; He is everywhere. Therefore, He can be enjoyed everywhere. I will not say that you cannot enjoy the Lord everywhere, but I am sure you cannot enjoy the Lord as the peace offering everywhere. You may enjoy the Lord in other aspects, but you cannot enjoy the Lord as the peace offering in any place but in the tent of meeting. This is exceedingly vital. To enjoy the peace offering is not to be done at home, but absolutely in the tent of meeting.

THE BLOOD AROUND
THE ALTAR

The third point concerns the shedding of the blood. The offering was killed on the altar by the presenter, and then the priest sprinkled the blood around the altar. We all know that the altar symbolizes the cross, and the killing of the offering symbolizes the Lord's death. But the blood of the peace offering was not to be brought into the Holiest of All; it was to be sprinkled around the altar where the peace offering was enjoyed. It was not for God, but for the presenter, for when the presenter looked at the blood, he immediately had peace.

We know that Satan, the accuser, is always busy. He never sleeps. Wherever we are, there he is, and he is even with us now. He is always accusing the hearts and minds of the saints. Sometimes he says, "What are you doing here in this meeting? Don't you remember how you lost your temper this morning? Don't you remember what you did today? You have no right to be here." What shall we do when the accuser comes to us in such a way? Praise the Lord for the blood! We must not only apply the blood, but also point the enemy to the blood. We must say, "Satan, look at the blood! You ask me to look at my failures, but I ask you to look at the blood!" When we do this, there is real peace.

But sometimes we are not so bold. Immediately after Satan accuses us, we pray, "O Lord, have mercy upon me and forgive me." Is this right or wrong? It is absolutely wrong! Do not pray or confess, but declare to Satan that the blood is here. "Satan, look at the blood! You ask me to look at my failures and my sinfulness, but I demand you to look at the blood!" This really gives us peace. We have the blood of Christ, and the blood gives us peace. Hallelujah! We do have an altar for the shedding of the blood, and we have the sprinkling of the blood around the altar. This is the peace offering.

How many times have you applied the blood in this way? I am afraid that many, many times we have applied the blood in a begging way, not in a way of declaration and proclamation. Moreover, it is not necessary for us to claim; we must simply proclaim: "Satan, look at the blood!" Would we be so bold? If we practice this, we will have peace.

TWO COLUMNS OF THE PEACE OFFERING

The fourth point concerning the peace offering is that it is built upon the previous offerings. "And Aaron's sons shall burn it on the altar upon the burnt offering, which is upon the wood that is on the fire: it is an offering made by fire, of a sweet savor unto the Lord....If he present it for a thanksgiving, then he shall present with the sacrifice of thanksgiving unleavened cakes mingled with oil, and unleavened wafers anointed with oil, and cakes mingled with oil, of fine flour, soaked. Besides the cakes, he shall present for his offering leavened bread with the sacrifice of thanksgiving of his peace offerings" (Lev. 3:5; 7:12-13, lit.).

The peace offering is built upon two columns of the burnt offering and the meal offering. The two foregoing offerings are the base of the peace offering. We all must realize that though there are five kinds of offerings, yet only two are the base: the burnt offering and the meal offering. These two are the basic offerings upon which the following offerings are built. According to Leviticus 3:5, the peace offering must be burned upon the burnt offering. If we do not have the burnt offering, we have no place to burn the peace offering. The burnt offering is a base for burning the peace offering. Then Leviticus 7:12-13 shows us that the meal offering is also necessary for presenting the peace offering.

What does this mean? It simply means that we must first experience Christ as the burnt offering and then as the meal offering. Then upon these experiences we may have the experience of Christ as the peace offering. If we are going to offer Christ as the peace offering, we need many experiences of Christ as the meal offering. The more we experience Christ as the meal offering by enjoying His humanity, the more we will enjoy Him as the peace offering. Hence, the experience of the peace offering is based mainly upon the burnt offering and the meal offering.

A FEAST OF JOY

The fifth point is that the peace offering is a matter of joy. "Also in the day of your gladness, and in your set feasts, and in the beginnings of your new moons, ye shall blow with the trumpets over your burnt offerings, and over the sacrifices of your peace offerings; that they may be to you for a memorial before your God: I am the Lord your God." "And thou shalt present peace offerings, and shalt eat there, and rejoice before the Lord thy God" (Num. 10:10; Deut. 27:7, lit.). The peace offering is a joy and a feast. It is a little different from the burnt offering and the meal offering. It is absolutely a matter of joy and feasting.

First Corinthians 10:18 refers to the peace offering, for it says that the people of Israel ate the sacrifices and were partakers of the altar. By the following verses in this chapter, we can realize that presenting Christ to God as the peace offering today is to come to the Lord's table. When we come to the Lord's table, that is the time to present Christ to God as our peace offering. And the Lord's table is a joyful feast. Whenever we come to the Lord's table, we come to enjoy a feast. We will see more concerning this later.

THE FELLOWSHIP
OF FIVE PARTIES

God Himself

The sixth point is that the peace offering is the fellowship of God's people with God and with one another. In Leviticus 3 and 7, we are told clearly how many parties have the right to enjoy the peace offering. The first party that enjoys the peace offering is God. All the fat, the inwards with the kidneys, and the net over the liver belong to God. All of these tender parts are God's portion. These verses tell us clearly that these parts are food to God. He is the first party to enjoy the peace offering.

The Serving Priest

The second party to enjoy the peace offering is the serving priest who sprinkles the blood and offers the fat unto God. The serving priest enjoys the right shoulder (the right foreleg) and one of each kind of the cakes of the meal offering. All these pieces are called the heave offering, which signifies the ascended Christ. To "heave" signifies to ascend. The ascended Christ is the heave offering, and this is the highest enjoyment of Christ. The serving priest enjoys Christ in these pieces as the ascended One.

The Priesthood

The third party to enjoy the peace offering is the priesthood. Aaron and his sons have the breast as their portion. The leg (the shoulder) signifies the walking strength, and the breast signifies the embracing love. The priesthood can enjoy the embracing love of the peace offering. This is called the wave offering. The wave offering signifies Christ in resurrection. These points are all very meaningful.

The Presenter

The fourth party to enjoy the peace offering is the presenter. The one who presents the offering enjoys the flesh, that is, the meat. All the flesh is for the enjoyment of the one who offers the peace offering.

All the Cleansed Ones

But there is also a fifth party. All the people of God who are clean are also entitled to enjoy the peace offering. "But the soul that eateth of the flesh of the sacrifice of peace offerings, that pertain unto the Lord, having his uncleanness upon him, even that soul shall be cut off from his people. Moreover the soul that shall touch any unclean thing, as the uncleanness of man, or any unclean beast, or any abominable unclean thing, and eat of the flesh of the sacrifice of peace offerings, which pertain unto the

Lord, even that soul shall be cut off from his people" (Lev. 7:20-21). All the clean ones among the children of God are entitled to enjoy the peace offering. This is Christ in the Lord's table meeting. At the Lord's table, Christ is our peace offering.

Coming to the Lord's table is a declaration to the whole universe that we have peace with God. It is also a declaration that we have peace with all the saints. If I do not have peace with a certain brother, it is rather difficult for me to come to the Lord's table in a true way. To come to the Lord's table is to declare that we have peace with God and peace with one another. We have peace with all the priesthood, and we even have peace with ourselves. We have peace with all the saints, so we are in the feast enjoying Christ as our peace offering. There is a part for God, a part for the serving ones, a part for the priesthood, a great part for the presenter, and also a part for all the saints. This is our real communion. Our communion is simply Christ as the peace offering for God's enjoyment, for the serving one's enjoyment, for the priesthood's enjoyment, for our enjoyment, and for the enjoyment of all the saints.

The proper way to have the Lord's table is not simply a matter of singing hymns, praising, and praying while taking the bread and the wine. It is absolutely a matter of having the full enjoyment for these five parties. There must be the enjoyment for God, for the serving ones, for the priesthood, for the presenter, and for all the attendants who are clean. In other words, the Lord's table meeting is a matter of enjoyment, so it is a feast full of gladness.

BLOWING THE TRUMPET

Numbers 10:10 tells us that we should blow the trumpet over the sacrifice of our peace offering. What does it mean to blow the trumpet? It simply means to declare and to proclaim. The trumpet was a picture, and the fulfillment is to proclaim. We need to proclaim to the whole universe, "Look all of you angels, demons, and even the Devil! Look at the peaceful enjoyment that we have here! As the redeemed ones, we have peace with God, we have peace with one another, and we even have peace with ourselves. We are enjoying Christ in the presence of God and with one another!"

I do not believe that many Christians today have fully realized to such an extent what the Lord's table is. We all must realize that the Lord's table is a feast with Christ as the peace offering for all five parties to enjoy. God is here, the serving ones are here, the priests are here, and the presenters with all the children of God are here. When all five parties are together we do not sit inactively, but trumpet and proclaim to the universe, "What a Christ we have!" He is our peace, not only in an objective way, but as our enjoyment. We are enjoying peace, and this peace is Christ.

Christ as the peace offering is not like manna sent from the heavens. This offering is something that we must bring to the tent of meeting. What we bring to the meeting is the very Christ whom we have experienced as the burnt offering and the meal offering. After experiencing Christ in such a way, we have something of Him to bring to the meeting to offer to God as the peace offering for a mutual enjoyment for all the five parties. This is the presentation and the enjoyment of the peace offering, and this is a full portrait of the Lord's table.

GOD'S PORTION

God's portion of the peace offering is the hidden part. He gets all the inwards with all the fat and the two kidneys. This is indeed meaningful. We cannot understand the "inwards" of Christ. We can present them, but we cannot appreciate them so deeply. The inwards of Christ can only be understood, apprehended, and appreciated by God Himself. They are too deep, too hidden, and too mysterious to us. Yet, praise the Lord, we can present them! We cannot appreciate them so deeply, and we cannot apprehend the mystery, but we can present them to God and let God enjoy this hidden part.

What does Christ think within Himself? What does He consider deep in His being? No one can realize such depths; therefore, not one of us can enjoy this part. We are not qualified, but God is qualified; so this is His part. The hidden and mysterious part of Christ is for God, and this is God's food. God is satisfied by the inwards of Christ who is offered by us. Every time we have the Lord's table, it is also a dining table for God. Some of us have been meeting in the local church and enjoying the Lord's table for years, but I do not believe that many of us have realized that the Lord's table is also a dining table for God. It is not only the saints who come and dine, but God also who comes and dines. It is here that we present something to God which is so hidden and mysterious that we cannot apprehend it. But God can! This is the inward parts of Christ, the most tender and precious parts of His inner being. All the fat of the inwards and all the tender, sweet, and precious parts are for God's appreciation and God's enjoyment. Leviticus 3 mentions repeatedly that this is God's food.

THE SERVING ONES' PORTION

The serving ones enjoy the right shoulder, that is, the right front leg. This means that the more I serve in this way, the more I will have the strength to walk as Christ walks. He simply becomes my right leg for walking. The serving ones also have the right to participate in one of each kind of the cakes. The right leg and the cakes together constitute the heave offering, which is Christ in ascension. The leg, as we have pointed out, signifies the walking strength, and the different kinds of cakes signify the rich nourishment and satisfaction. In the next Lord's table meeting, some will be the serving ones in the meeting, and all of them will have the realization that while they are serving, they are enjoying Christ in His ascension. Christ is their walking strength, and their rich nourishment and full satisfaction.

The breast, which is the embracing strength in love, is for the priesthood. All the priests have the right to enjoy the embracing love of Christ in resurrection.

The flesh of the offering is for the presenter and for all the people in the tent of meeting who are clean. Hence, if we are serving ones, we not only have a special right to enjoy the right shoulder and one of each kind of the cakes, but we also have the right to enjoy the breast, because we are in the priesthood. In addition to this, we have the right to enjoy the flesh, because we are one of the clean ones among God's people. The serving ones have the right to enjoy everything but God's portion, which is too deep and too mysterious for them. They have the full right to enjoy all the other parts.

Sometimes when we come to the tent of meeting, we are clean, but we do not present anything. We may be a presenter, yet not a priest. In position we are all priests, but in the church some will not function as the priests. Only the functioning ones in the meeting are the priesthood. All the rest are just the attendants. Thus, in a sense, we may be clean, yet we are not in the priesthood. We may even be in the priesthood, yet not so active as a serving one. We must not only be the clean ones, but also the presenters, the priesthood, and the serving ones. Then we will have the full right to enjoy Christ in so many ways as the peace offering.

THE UNCLEAN ONES

Besides these five parties, there is still another party, the cut-off ones. "But the soul that eateth of the flesh of the sacrifice of peace offerings, that pertain unto the Lord, having his uncleanness upon him, even that soul shall be cut off from his people" (Lev. 7:20). The unclean ones are cut off. The fulfillment of this type is seen in 1 Corinthians 5:9-11: "I wrote unto you in an epistle not to company with fornicators: yet not altogether with the fornicators of this world, or with the covetous, or extortioners, or with idolaters; for then must ye needs go out of the world. But now I have written unto you not to keep company, if any man that is called a brother be a fornicator, or covetous, or an idolater, or a railer, or a drunkard, or an extortioner; with such a one, no, not to eat."

The unclean ones must be cut off from the church fellowship, and that is the meaning of the term "excommunication." The unclean members of the church must be excommunicated from the church fellowship. So we see that it is a serious thing to come to the fellowship of the Lord's table. It is a joyful feast on the one hand, but on the other hand the Lord's table is a most holy thing. Whenever we come to participate in the fellowship of the Lord's table, we must realize that this is a holy matter. We are not only fellowshipping with others, but also with God. It is not simply man that is enjoying this table, but also God. God is feasting together with us; hence, how can a person that is unclean participate in the peace offering? That is a kind of insult to the Lord. Therefore, the unclean persons must be cut off until they become clean again.

THE NEED OF DAILY EXPERIENCES

We have seen from the peace offering the real meaning of the Lord's table. It is a feast set before God and before the saints in the church, with Christ as our peace offering for the enjoyment of all the parties involved. But there is one matter that we must stress. The peace offering that we bring to the church meetings to present to God depends upon our daily experiences of Christ as our burnt offering and meal offering. For the Lord's table meeting, we need more and more proper and adequate experiences of Christ in these two aspects, especially in the humanity of Jesus. This is why we spent so much time to consider the meal offering. The humanity of Jesus is very basic in our experience in order for us to bring the peace offering to the Lord's table.

CHAPTER NINETEEN

THE PEACE OFFERING
AND THE LORD'S TABLE

Scripture Reading: Lev. 7:14-21, 29-34; 1 Cor. 10:16-18, 21; 5:11-13

THE NEED OF CLEANSING

The peace offering always mentions the sprinkling of the blood. As we have pointed out, the sprinkling of the blood in the peace offering is not within the holiest of all, but around the altar where the people enjoy and partake of the peace offering. This is because when we enjoy Christ, we need the sprinkling of the blood. The children of Israel did not have the right to enjoy the passover lamb without the sprinkling of the blood upon the outside of the house (Exo. 12:7-8). This signifies that the enjoyment of Christ is under the covering of the blood. Whenever we come to the Lord's table, we must realize that we need the covering of His redeeming and cleansing blood. We have no merit to come to the Lord's table without His blood.

By reading 1 Corinthians 10 carefully, we realize that the Apostle Paul's intention was to show us that the altar in ancient times was a type of the Lord's table in New Testament times. The people of Israel had the altar, but today we have the table. They had communion over the altar, and we have communion over the table. Our table is the altar, and their altar was the table. In the type of the altar, we see clearly that the blood was sprinkled around all four sides of the altar. While they were enjoying something on the altar, they could see the sprinkling of the blood from every side.

Today the principle is the same. Whenever we come to our altar, the Lord's table, to enjoy and partake of the Lord, we must realize that we need the sprinkling of His blood. Several times the saints have asked me why I always mention the blood when I am praising the Lord around His table. I have been asked this question not only in this country, but also in other countries. If you were to ask me the same question, I would know that you do not realize the need of the cleansing blood. No doubt we are already cleansed, but we still need cleansing all the time. We are still in this flesh, and our flesh is fallen. Regardless of how good, how nice, how pure, and how clean you consider your flesh, it is still filthy and fallen. Even if we do not have the consciousness that we are filthy, the flesh is still filthy. No flesh can be justified by the holy God. Therefore, whenever we come to contact the Lord, we need the cleansing blood.

Some may say they have been victorious for many months, and during all this time they did not lose their temper once. Because of this, they may consider that they are very clean and pure. But no matter how good we think we are, we all need the cleansing of the blood for the enjoyment of Christ. Hence, whenever we come to the Lord's table, we need to apply the blood. To come to the Lord's table is absolutely different from coming to a restaurant table. The things on the table in the restaurant are common, but the things on the Lord's table are holy. We, on the other hand, are so unclean. In order to contact these holy things, we need the cleansing of the blood. Whenever we come to the Lord's table, we must apply the cleansing of the blood for the enjoyment of the Lord.

THE DIFFERENCE IN APPRECIATION

Another point concerning the peace offering is the difference in the appreciation of the Lord. This is seen in the different sizes of the offerings. Some might offer

a cow, a large offering. Others might offer a lamb, which
is smaller. Still others might offer a goat. We all know
that in the Bible a goat is not good. Sheep are good, but
goats are not good (see Matt. 25:32-33). Why then does
the Bible present something which is not so good as a
type of Christ? Christ, of course, is always good, but
sometimes those of us who are the presenters of Christ
are not so good. We are not like a lamb, but rather like
a goat with two horns. Moreover, a goat is rather wild;
it is not mild like a lamb. There are times when we
realize that the dear one who is offering Christ as the
peace offering to God is rather wild. There is the feeling
that this presenter is just like a wild goat. He is not
gentle like a lamb, but he is rather like a goat.

Christ Himself is the same. He is the same yesterday,
today, and forever. But there can be a difference in our
presentation and appreciation of Christ. He is different
in the offering not because of Himself, but because of us.
Sometimes we appreciate Christ as a large cow and
sometimes as a little lamb. But I am afraid that most of
the time our appreciation of Christ is rather wild and is
just like a goat. So we need some improvement. The Lord
does not need any improvement, but we need improvement.

There is a real difference in the apprehension, experience, and appreciation of Christ. Therefore, there is a
difference in the presentation of Christ. What we offer
in the church meetings depends very much upon our daily
experience of Christ. If in our daily walk we experience
Christ in a certain way, then surely when we come to the
church meeting, we will present Christ in that way. If
we experience Christ in our daily walk in a mild way,
then surely we will present Christ in the meeting in that
way. But if we experience Christ daily in a wild way,
then, of course, we can only present Christ in the meeting
in the same way. What we present in the meetings
depends upon what we enjoy and experience in our daily

life. If we enjoy Him more, then we can present more. If we enjoy Him less, then we will present less.

We all know that in Christianity, most of the so-called services do not depend upon the presenter. In a sense, they may not have any presenters. Mainly, they have simply the pew members. Since they do not have any presenters, their meetings do not depend upon the members, but upon the speaker. If they have a good speaker, then they consider that a good service. If they have a poor speaker, that is a poor service. But the church meeting is different. The meetings of the church do not depend upon a speaker, but entirely upon the presenters. We may even have a poor speaker, yet the church can still have the very best meeting. This is because in the church all the presenters are the rich ones. Now we can realize that the church meeting is not a Christianity service, but an enjoyable feast of all those who apprehend, experience, and appreciate Christ. They bring the Christ whom they experience to their meeting and present Him to God, and this portion is God's food.

THE WAVE BREAST AND HEAVE SHOULDER

With the peace offering there is also the wave breast and the heave shoulder. The shoulder here, as we have mentioned, means the leg. The breast is the loving part, and the leg is the strengthening part. The leg is not only for walking, but also for standing. Our standing strength depends upon our two legs. When we are weak, we simply cannot stand. But as long as we can stand, we are sound and strong. This is why the heave offering is so transcendent and powerful.

The breast is the wave offering in resurrection. The love of Christ is really living and weighty. So we have the breast as the loving part of Christ and the shoulder as the strengthening part of Christ. The shoulder is only for the serving priest, and the breast is for all the priesthood. The wave breast is loving and tender, but it is not as strong as the leg. This is why the leg is for the ministering priest. Then the meat of the peace offering is for the presenter, and there is also a portion for the presenter to share with all the clean ones.

PRACTICAL, NOT DOCTRINAL, PRIESTS

Suppose we are the people of Israel and we are having a feast in the tent of meeting. There must be some who are the presenters, and surely some should be the priests. In the Old Testament times some were priests and some were people, but today in the church all are priests. But this can be merely doctrinal and not practical. In doctrine we all are priests, but in practice perhaps only two out of ten are the actual priests. There are some who are just like the common people of Israel, because in the church meeting they do not function. I am afraid that too many attend the meeting with the desire and expectation to get something. They listen to the message and the testimonies, but they never realize that they must serve in the meeting as a functioning priest.

But there are a number of brothers and sisters who do put their shoulder under the ark of the meetings of the church. They pray and are burdened for the meetings all day long, and when the time comes for the meeting, they are more and more burdened. Therefore, when they come to the meeting, they come to bear something, not just with the expectation to get something. When the meeting seems to be going down, they immediately exercise their spirit to pray that the Lord will uplift the meeting. They are ministering by bearing the responsibility; so they are the active priesthood. Whenever there is an offering in the meeting, these dear ones surely will enjoy the breast as the priesthood. They will enjoy the loving, tender part.

Then from among the active serving ones who are the actual priesthood, there might be two or three who are ministering as I am doing now. I am the present serving one, burning the fat to the Lord. I am the one who sprinkles the blood on the altar. Therefore, I have the right to enjoy the breast, the shoulder, and the extra pieces of the different cakes. I have the right to enjoy the wave offering and the heave offering. As a member of the priesthood, I enjoy the wave breast, and as a serving one, I can also enjoy the heave shoulder and the heave cakes. The more you serve, the more you enjoy. The less you serve, the less you enjoy. If you are not in the actual priesthood, you are just one among the people, and you miss the right to enjoy the wave breast. And, of course, if you are not presently serving, you have no right to enjoy the heave shoulder and the heave cakes.

So we all must be the attendants presenting something in the meeting. We all must bring something as a peace offering to the feast of the church. There is no way that we can borrow an offering from others. What we bring depends entirely upon our experience and appreciation of Christ in our daily life. Day by day, hour after hour, we must spend much time on Christ that we may have a real harvest of Christ. Then when we come to the meeting, we will have something of Christ to present to God as a peace offering. The hidden part is for God's satisfaction; the loving part is for the stronger ones; the strengthening part is for the serving ones; and the major part is for all the clean ones. If we all will be faithful in this way, how rich and uplifting our meetings will be, and how different they will be from today's Christian meetings. I do look to the Lord that all the meetings in the local churches will be like this.

THE DIFFERENCE IN MOTIVE AND FEELING

Now we must see something more concerning the peace offering. In the appreciation of Christ, there is another kind of difference. Not only is there a difference in size, but also a difference in feeling. Some peace offerings are offered as a thanksgiving, and some are offered for a voluntary vow. "And of it he shall present one cake out of each offering for a heave offering unto the Lord, and it shall be the priest's that sprinkleth the blood of the peace offerings. And the flesh of the sacrifice of his peace offerings for thanksgiving shall be eaten the same day that it is presented; he shall not leave any of it until the morning. But if the sacrifice of his offering be a vow, or a voluntary offering, it shall be eaten the same day that he presenteth his sacrifice; and on the morrow also the remainder of it shall be eaten" (Lev. 7:14-16, lit.).

Those who offer the peace offering for thanksgiving are very thankful to the Lord. The Lord has been very good to them, and they are grateful and thankful to the Lord. Therefore, they bring to the Lord a peace offering for thanksgiving. But let me ask a question: Do you think that this kind of offering is very strong in feeling? I believe that most of you might say yes, but I say no. This is the weakest feeling. For me to bring a peace offering to the Lord because He has been so good to me is more or less like making a bargain with the Lord. When Jacob was young, he made a bargain with the Lord like this. He told the Lord that if He would provide for his eating, his clothing, his housing, and protection, then he would do certain things for the Lord (Gen. 28:20-22). It is easy to be thankful to the Lord when He is so good to you. But suppose the Lord is not so good to you. How would you feel then? Some may get a better job, some a better home, some a better car, and some a better degree. Everything is better all the time. Then they will be very thankful to the Lord, and they will come to the meeting with a peace offering for thanksgiving. There is a feeling in this peace offering, but it is not a very strong feeling.

Suppose that when you look for a better home, you eventually get one that is worse. And when you look for a better job, you don't find it, and instead, you lose your present job. What would you do then? Could you still come to the meeting with a peace offering? I don't think so. You simply will not have the peace. But there is another kind of peace offering. This is a peace offering for a voluntary vow. Those who give this offering do not care whether the Lord gives them a better home or not. In fact, they don't care whether the Lord gives them anything. They are just here for the Lord's recovery. This is a vow to them. The heavens and the earth can flee away, but they are still for the Lord's recovery. Undoubtedly, this kind of feeling is very strong.

Many times in the meetings, we hear these two kinds of peace offerings. Some offer a peace offering of thanksgiving by saying, "Praise the Lord, He is so good to me. I only expected to get a job paying $400.00 a month, but now I have one that pays $550.00 a month." Sometimes, on the other hand, we hear some of the saints say, "Hallelujah! Praise the Lord! We don't care for this and we don't care for that! We are just here for the Lord's recovery! Lord, what a mercy that we could be here for You!" This is a vow, and it is voluntary. We may lose our job, we may lose many things, yet we are so strong.

The peace offering for thanksgiving is only good to eat for one day. It cannot last longer; it immediately becomes old. "Hallelujah, I have a better car, and the Lord gave me such a good home. I did not ask for this much, but He gave it to me." This kind of offering is only fresh for the present meeting. Tomorrow it will be old. After we have told the church that the Lord gave us such a good job, we cannot repeat it tomorrow. If we repeat it again tomorrow, no one will listen. It will stink because it is too old. But a peace offering of a vow is good for three days. We can repeat it the next day, and we can repeat it again.

Thus, the peace offering for thanksgiving is much weaker than the peace offering for the voluntary vow. The voluntary vow is stronger and lasts longer. The difference is in our motive and in our feeling. What kind of motive do we have when we bring Christ into the meeting? Do we only have the motive of thanksgiving, or do we have the motive of a vow? We all must learn to bring Christ to the meeting for a vow. Regardless of whether or not He would do anything for us, we are still for Him. Even if He puts us in prison as He did John the Baptist, we will still praise Him. John was very strong in testifying for Christ, but when he was put into prison, he sent his disciples to ask the Lord if He was really the Christ. In other words, he was saying that if Jesus were really the Christ, He would get him out of prison. But the Lord Jesus told John's disciples to tell John that He did many things for the blind and the lame, but He would not do one thing for him. He added that John will be blessed if he is not offended. If we would be offended when the Lord treats us in this way, then we could only offer a peace offering for thanksgiving. We could never offer a peace offering for a vow.

Suppose a young sister who has been hoping for a baby boy for a number of years finally has her "Isaac." I do believe that this young mother will bring a peace offering of thanksgiving to the meeting. But suppose that after six months, the Lord takes away her "Isaac." Will this sister still bring a peace offering of thanksgiving to the meeting? I am afraid that it will be a weeping offering. If we are here simply for the Lord to do something for us, we can only offer the peace offering of thanksgiving. But if we are here for the Lord, with a voluntary vow for His purpose, we do have a strong motive to bring as a peace offering to the meeting. This offering always lasts longer.

Together with this point, there is another aspect. In the presentation of the peace offering, we always need to offer something new and fresh. We should not offer the peace offering which we offered yesterday. We need something new for today. Every day we need some new experiences of Christ. We all must realize that it is not so good to apply our old appreciations of Christ. It is really poor to apply what we experienced two months ago, and it is also not good to apply something of yesterday. We always need some fresh and new peace offerings.

THE HOLY PEACE OFFERING

Now we come to the last point. The peace offering is holy. This is why the Lord's table is really a holy communion. We all must be holy. If we are unclean, we must be cut off from the communion and fellowship of the Body. The peace offering was a type, and the fellowship around the Lord's table is the fulfillment of this type. First Corinthians 10 tells us that the Lord's table is the fulfillment of the enjoyment of the peace offering, and in chapter five of the same book, Paul tells us that all unclean persons should be put away from the fellowship of the church.

Who are the unclean persons? Paul makes it clear that fornicators are the first ones. Nothing is so dirty and abominable in the eyes of God as fornication. This is a damage and confusion to the proper humanity. It is really unclean in the eyes of God. Those who are involved in fornication must be put away unless they repent and have a real turn to the Lord, applying His precious blood to cleanse away the uncleanness. Otherwise, such unclean persons should never touch the Lord's table. Paul is even stronger than this. He says that we should not keep company with such unclean persons. Of course, we do not like to have any legal regulations, but many times when I have come to the Lord's table, I have prayed very much that the Lord would take care of His table. He is the only One who knows the real unclean persons. But we all are responsible to the Lord. It is not a small matter to defile the Lord's table.

We all must take this matter seriously to the Lord. If we have become involved in some kind of uncleanness, the Lord is merciful and gracious; He is willing to forgive and cleanse us, yet we need to repent. We need to return to the Lord and have a clear dealing and apply the Lord's blood upon our uncleanness. Otherwise, we are unclean. If we come to the Lord's table when we are unclean, we do not have fellowship within. Deep within, in our spirit, we are cut off already, because we are unclean or we have touched something unclean. There is some uncleanness upon us. We ourselves may be clean, but the Word says that if we touch something unclean or someone unclean, we are defiled. Therefore, we need to repent, make confession, and apply the Lord's blood. Some brothers and sisters may become involved in fornication, and if we talk to them in detail about all these things, we too become unclean. We need then to have a thorough cleansing by applying the Lord's blood.

Paul said in 1 Corinthians 10:21: "Ye cannot drink the cup of the Lord, and the cup of devils: ye cannot be partakers of the Lord's table, and of the table of devils." "Devils" in this verse means demons. We cannot partake of the Lord's table and at the same time partake of something of the demons.

It is very good to have the church meetings as a feast for us all to offer something to God. But there is another aspect which is quite serious. We should never come to the Lord's table when we are unclean. We must be cleansed by the Lord's blood and have a complete repentance and dealing with the Lord.

In 1 Corinthians 5 Paul speaks of six sinful things that make us unclean, and in the next chapter he mentions several unclean things again. But he says, "Such were some of you: but ye are washed...in the name of the Lord Jesus, and by the Spirit of our God" (1 Cor. 6:11). So many of us were very sinful, but we are washed; we are cleansed by His precious blood, in His mighty name, and by His Spirit. But if we are still living in some of these unclean things without a real repentance and a real dealing with the Lord, then we are unclean and unworthy to come to the Lord's table. May the Lord have mercy upon all of us!

CHAPTER TWENTY

THE EXPERIENCE OF CHRIST AS OUR SIN OFFERING

Scripture Reading: Lev. 4:1-15, 22-28, 32; 6:25-30; 2 Cor. 5:21a; Rom. 8:3b; Heb. 9:12; 13:11-12

FIVE OFFERINGS

This chapter will cover the sin offering, which is the fourth kind of offering. When discussing the first offering, we pointed out why the five kinds of offerings were needed. It is because, in the presence of God, we are in five kinds of situations or conditions. We were made for God, but we are not for God. Therefore, we need Christ as the One who is absolutely for God as our burnt offering. Neither are we fine or perfect or properly balanced. Hence, we need Christ as the meal offering, because He is so fine, so perfect, and so balanced in His humanity. Also, we have no peace with God or with others. In the whole universe there is no peace, and among human beings there is no peace. In the schools there is no peace; in society there is no peace; among the nations there is no peace. Though we have the United Nations, there is still no peace. There is no peace in the homes between husbands and wives and between children and parents. We do not have peace with God, and we do not have peace with one another. So we need Christ as our peace offering.

Then we are sinful. And even more than that, we are sin. We are just sin itself. So we need Christ as our sin offering. And because we are sin, we are full of mistakes and wrongdoings. There is nothing right with us. We are wrong with our parents; we are wrong with our husband; we are wrong with our wife; we are wrong with our brothers; we are wrong with our sisters; we are wrong with our children; we are wrong with everyone! Even in the way we dress and cut our hair we are wrong. We are wrong in every aspect. At one time in the past I was dealing with the Lord about certain things. I thought that about an hour would be enough time to get through. But I soon discovered that I was wrong in everything. There was nothing in which I was right. Therefore, we need Christ as our trespass offering.

This is our condition before God. We are not for God; we are not fine and perfect; we have no peace with God and man; we are just sin itself; and we are full of mistakes and wrongdoings. These are our five conditions, so we need five kinds of offerings. But, praise the Lord! This means that we can apply Christ in at least five aspects. He is just the One that we need. We are not for God, but He is. We are not perfect, but He is. We do not have peace, but He is peace. We are sinful; we are sin, but He is the sin offering to deal with our sin. And we are full of mistakes, but He is our trespass offering. Hallelujah! We have such a Christ, who takes care of all our situations before God.

We should not consider that we are such wonderful persons. Not one among us is wonderful. In fact, we are pitiful. We are not for God; we are still for ourselves. We have mentioned the matter of thanksgiving and the vow in the last chapter. We are for thanksgiving; we are not for a vow. This indicates that we are so much for ourselves. We have no concern for God. We are not perfect and fine, and we really do not have peace. Our mind is not a mind for God; it is a mind for sin. The more we consider ourselves in the light, the more we find that there is nothing but sin. But, praise the Lord, we are so much negatively, and Christ is so much positively! Whatever we are not, He is. We can enjoy Him as the burnt offering and as the meal offering. These are the two basic offerings.

And based upon these offerings, we can enjoy Him as our peace offering.

SIN

But there is something more that we need to see. At the time we repented to take the Lord Jesus as our Savior, we did not realize that we were so sinful. We may have realized that we were not so good and that we had done many wrong things, but we never realized that we are just sin itself. Whether we intend to do something sinful or we do not intend to do something sinful, we are just sin. Therefore, the word "unwittingly" is used in Leviticus 4. "And the Lord spake unto Moses, saying, Speak unto the children of Israel, saying, If a soul shall sin unwittingly against any of the commandments of the Lord concerning things which ought not to be done, and shall do against any of them: if the priest that is anointed do sin so as to bring guilt on the people; then let him bring for his sin, which he hath sinned, a young bullock without blemish unto the Lord for a sin offering" (Lev. 4:1-3, lit.).

For this word "unwittingly" we could also use "unwillingly," "ignorantly," "unaware," or "inadvertently." This is a picture, and it means that we must realize while we are enjoying the Lord as our burnt offering, meal offering, and peace offering, we are just sin. Regardless of whether we have the intention of hating others or not, eventually we will hate them. Whether we are willing to lose our temper or not, we will simply lose it. We may not even like to be proud, but we will certainly be proud. This is what Paul is talking about in Romans 7. He says that the things he hates to do, that is what he does. He does not want to do it, yet he does it. Perhaps in the morning we make a decision not to gossip at all that day. But during the day we gossip more than ever. We make a decision not to criticize others anymore, yet an hour later we are very critical of someone. Paul says in Romans 7:17, "Now it is no longer I that do it, but sin that dwells in me." It is not I, but sin. In Galatians 2:20, we have this word: "No longer I who live, but Christ lives in me." Romans 7 says that it is not I, but sin. It is another person as in Galatians 2:20, but this person's name is not Christ; this person's name is sin. His first name is sin, his last name is sin, and his middle name is also sin. Sin! Sin! Sin! "Now it is no longer I that do it, but sin that dwells in me."

We may think that we are doing a wonderful deed, but eventually we may discover that what we had done was terrible. At the time we did it, we thought it was wonderful. But it turned out to be awful. What does this prove? It simply proves that within us there is something called sin, and this sin is just ourselves.

THE SOURCE

Leviticus 4 is very difficult for people to understand. When I was a young Christian, I tried for many years to understand this chapter, but I failed to do so. First of all, this chapter says that if a priest does something wrong unwittingly, he must offer the sin offering. Then it says that if the congregation of the Lord's people does something unwittingly, they must offer the sin offering. Later it says that if a ruler among the people does something wrong unwittingly, he must offer the sin offering. And it even mentions that if a common person does anything wrong unwittingly, he must offer the sin offering. By this picture, we can realize that this is a congregation that is worshiping and serving God, which is exactly what we are doing today. We are simply a congregation that worships God by enjoying Christ as our burnt offering, meal offering, and peace offering. We may think that we are getting along quite well. We are in the recovery of the church life, so whatever we do surely must be right. However, it may seem right today, but after three weeks, we may discover that what we did three weeks ago was horrible.

This chapter first mentions that the leading serving

one may do something wrong. Yet he may think that it is one hundred percent correct. He does it unwittingly. After a certain time, he discovers that it was wrong. What is this? This is not a kind of mistake. This is something out of our inner being. Our inward being is just sin; therefore, what comes out cannot be right. This chapter goes on to say that the whole congregation, a ruler in the congregation, or a common person in the congregation may do something wrong. All of these persons do something wrong unwittingly. The picture here shows us that within us there is something that always causes us to be wrong. This chapter does not deal with mistakes or wrong doing; it deals with the source of our mistakes.

What is the source of our mistakes? We may say that it is sin, but this can be just a doctrinal answer. We must realize that *we* are the source of all our mistakes. If there were no one in the local church, surely the local church would never make any mistakes. But the more brothers and sisters there are, the more mistakes will be made. If we had only ten brothers and sisters meeting together, surely the mistakes could never be as many as we have today; today we have almost one thousand sources. This chapter does not deal with mistakes, but with the source of our mistakes. And that is our very self. We are just sin. Therefore, we need Christ as our sin offering. Within every drop of our blood and every fiber of our muscle is sin. We are simply constituted of sin. And because we are sin, we need a sin offering. Praise the Lord that Christ is our sin offering! Second Corinthians 5:21 says that Christ was made sin for us.

"CONCERNING SIN"

For many years after I was a Christian, I could not understand how Christ took away my sins. I was sinful, and I had committed many sins, yet Christ took away my sins by dying on the cross. Finally, after many years, I began to understand something concerning Christ bearing away our sins. But it was a much longer time before I could understand how Christ was made sin. He not only bore our sins, but He also was made sin. God made Him sin for us. When He died on the cross, He not only bore our sins, but He was there as sin. He was condemned and crucified there as sin. This is seen in Romans 8:3: "God sending His own Son in the likeness of the flesh of sin and concerning sin, condemned sin in the flesh." The phrase "concerning sin" could be adequately translated "as an offering for sin." It means that Christ became a sin offering to condemn sin. When Christ was crucified on the cross, He was crucified there not only as our Redeemer, but as sin itself. I realize that this is rather difficult for us to understand, but the type of the brass serpent gives us a good picture.

The Brass Serpent

The Lord Jesus told Nicodemus that He would be the brass serpent which Moses lifted up on a pole (John 3:14). We simply cannot understand. He was lifted up on the cross, and in our eyes He was Jesus, our Redeemer. But in God's eyes, He was there as the serpent. Of course, He was just the serpent in *form;* He did not have the *nature* of the serpent. The brass serpent was a serpent in form only, without the poison in it. Romans 8:3 says that God sent His Son in the likeness or in the form of the flesh of sin. He was in the form of the flesh of sin, yet He Himself had no sin. We must realize that Christ was made sin for us. We not only have many sins, but we are even sin itself. Therefore, Christ not only bore our sins, but He was also made sin for us. When He became flesh, He was made sin. Flesh in the Bible almost means sin. When Christ became flesh, He became sin. Since He was made sin, He could become our sin offering to deal with us as sin. He not only dealt with our sins, but He also dealt with us as sin.

THE BLOOD OF THE SIN OFFERING

The sin offering had to be killed by the presenter on

the altar in the presence of God. In this offering, the most important thing mentioned in detail is the blood. "And he shall bring the bullock unto the door of the tent of meeting before the Lord; and shall lay his hand upon the bullock's head, and kill the bullock before the Lord. And the priest that is anointed shall take of the bullock's blood, and bring it to the tent of meeting. And the priest shall dip his finger in the blood, and sprinkle of the blood seven times before the Lord, before the veil of the sanctuary. And the priest shall put some of the blood upon the horns of the altar of sweet incense before the Lord, which is in the tent of meeting; and shall pour all the blood of the bullock at the bottom of the altar of the burnt offering, which is at the door of the tent of meeting" (Lev. 4:4-7, lit.).

First the blood was shed; then the priest brought the blood into the holy place to sprinkle the blood seven times before the veil. This means that he sprinkled the blood seven times before God, who was behind the veil. There is no doubt that the purpose of this was to satisfy God's demand and requirement. Then after the sprinkling in the presence of God, the priest put some of the blood upon the four horns of the incense altar. We know that the incense altar is in the holy place, just before the veil, on the other side of which is God's presence in the Holiest of All. The blood is put on the four horns of the incense altar for our acceptance. The sprinkling of the blood seven times is for God's satisfaction, and the sprinkling of the blood on the four horns of the incense altar is for our acceptance. This means that whenever we come to have fellowship with God, we must do it by the merit of this blood. It is by this blood that our prayer and fellowship are accepted.

All the blood was then poured at the bottom of the altar in the sight of the presenter. By this time, the presenter is very much at peace because he realizes that the blood has been sprinkled before God, it has been placed on the horns of the incense altar, and it has been poured at the bottom of the altar. When he sees the blood, he realizes that he has been redeemed and fully accepted by God. All of His demands and requirements have been fulfilled by Christ. So the presenter is fully at peace. Because of this blood he has no fear. God has been fully satisfied, and he is fully accepted by God. The sprinkling of the blood seven times is for God, but the pouring out of the blood at the bottom of the altar is for the presenter.

Hebrews 9:12 tells us that when Christ ascended to the heavens, He brought His blood into the heavenly holy place, and He sprinkled the blood there. "Nor through the blood of goats and calves, but through His own blood, entered once for all into the Holy of Holies, having found an eternal redemption."

TWO KINDS OF SIN OFFERINGS

There are two kinds of sin offerings. One is for the priest who did wrong unwittingly, as well as for the whole congregation that did wrong unwittingly. For this sin offering, the blood must be brought into the sanctuary. But the blood of the sin offering for a ruler or for one of the common people need not be brought into the sanctuary. It was only necessary to put the blood on the four corners of the burnt offering altar to show forth the power and effectiveness of the blood as well as its redeeming and cleansing power. All the rest of the blood was then poured out at the bottom of the altar. Why is there the difference in these two sin offerings? In the first sin offering, the blood must be brought into the sanctuary to be sprinkled in the presence of God, but with the second, this was not necessary; the blood only needed to be put on the four horns of the burnt offering altar. This difference is because the first sin offering was for a congregation, but the second was for an individual. A congregation needs something of a more serious nature than an individual. No priest had the right to eat the first kind of sin offering; the whole offering was for God. But the priests did have the right to eat of the second kind of sin offering.

THE BODY OF THE SIN OFFERING

Now we must see something of the body of the sin offering. "And he shall take off from it all the fat of the bullock for the sin offering; the fat that covereth the inwards, and all the fat that is upon the inwards, and the two kidneys, and the fat that is upon them, which is by the flanks, and the net above the liver, with the kidneys, it shall he take away. As it was taken off from the bullock of the sacrifice of peace offerings: and the priest shall burn them upon the altar of the burnt offering. And the skin of the bullock, and all his flesh, with his head, and with his legs, and his inwards, and his dung, even the whole bullock shall he carry forth without the camp unto a clean place, where the ashes are poured out, and burn him on the wood with fire: where the ashes are poured out shall he be burnt" (Lev. 4:8-12, lit.).

These verses tell us clearly that the fat must be burned on the burnt offering altar as a sweet incense to God. This is for God's satisfaction. Then the whole body, including the skin, the inwards, and the dung is brought out of the camp to a clean place where the ashes are put. There the whole sin offering is burned. The fat must be burned on the burnt offering altar, but the rest of the body was burned outside the camp in a clean place where the ashes were put. There is a difference in the fat and the rest of the body because the fat is for God's satisfaction; therefore, it was burned on the altar. But the body is for God's righteous judgment, so it was burned in a place of judgment outside the camp.

The body of the sin offering for the congregation was absolutely God's portion. Nothing was for anyone else. But the sin offering for the individuals did leave a portion for the ministering priest. This shows us that Christ is so sufficient. He is sufficient to meet all the needs of the congregation, and He is more than sufficient to meet the need of individuals. As an individual, we can never exhaust Christ's sufficiency, so there is a portion left for the priests. If the sin offering is for the congregation, all is for God. But if the sin offering is for individuals, because individuals can never exhaust Christ, there is a part for others to enjoy.

THE WAY TO ENJOY THE SIN OFFERING

What is the way that the ministering priest enjoyed the portion of the sin offering? This is seen clearly in Leviticus 6:25-27a (lit.): "Speak unto Aaron and to his sons, saying, This is the law of the sin offering: In the place where the burnt offering is killed shall the sin offering be killed before the Lord: it is most holy. The priest that offereth it for sin shall eat it: in the holy place shall it be eaten, in the court of the tent of meeting. Whatsoever shall touch the flesh thereof shall be holy." First of all, it is clear that he could not enjoy the portion of the sin offering in his home. It must be enjoyed in the court of the tent of meeting. This kind of enjoyment of Christ belongs to the Body, the church; it is not an individual matter. You may enjoy Christ by yourself in a certain sense, but you can never enjoy Christ as the sin offering to God. This must be enjoyed in the court of the tent of meeting, and it must be enjoyed in a holy way.

BROKEN, SCOURED, AND RINSED

Now we must see something concerning the vessel which is used to boil the sin offering. "But the earthen vessel wherein it is boiled shall be broken: and if it be boiled in a brazen pot, it shall be both scoured, and rinsed in water" (Lev. 6:28, lit.). The earthen vessel must be broken, but if the vessel is of copper or brass, it must be scoured and rinsed. We are the earthen vessel. That is our natural being. We were made of the earth, so we are earthen vessels. The copper or brass in typology signifies God's judgment. This means that this kind of vessel has passed through God's judgment. Both the burnt offering altar and the laver were made of brass (Exo. 27:2; 30:18). So the brazen vessel represents our regenerated being. Our natural being is an earthen vessel, and our regenerated being is a brazen or copper vessel. Our natural being must be broken, and our regenerated being must be scoured and rinsed in water. This is the water in the Word mentioned in Ephesians 5:26. The scouring is the natural circumstances raised up by God to scour us. God uses the circumstances to scour us and His Word to rinse us. The natural part must be broken, and our regenerated part must be scoured and rinsed.

EATEN BY THE MALES

Only the males among the priests have the right to eat of the sin offering. The males always signify the stronger ones. Aaron had daughters, but they were not privileged to eat the sin offering. This indicates that only the stronger ones in the church life are privileged to eat Christ as the sin offering. When we minister Christ to others as the sin offering, this is a kind of gospel preaching. When we minister Christ as the sin offering in this way, we are a ministering priest. Thus, we are privileged to enjoy a portion of Christ as the sin offering. All the weaker ones in the church who do not minister Christ to others as the sin offering do not have the right to enjoy Christ as the sin offering. Only those who would minister Christ to others in this way are the stronger ones; therefore, they have the right and the position to enjoy Christ as the sin offering. Whether they are brothers or sisters, they are the males among the priests because they are the stronger ones in the church life.

DIFFERENCES IN SIZE

We also need to see the difference in the size of the sin offerings. A bullock is much stronger and more vigorous than a goat. The sin offering for the priest as well as the sin offering for the congregation was a young bullock. This signifies that Christ is so vigorous and full of strength that He can be the sin offering for a congregation. Then a male goat is mentioned which is much weaker and then

a female goat which is weaker still. Finally, there is a
female lamb which is the weakest. The sin offering may
be weaker or it may be stronger. Therefore, as with the
other offerings, there are degrees in the appreciation and
apprehension of Christ as the sin offering.

THE BLOOD AND THE ASHES

Two things remain in the sin offering as a strong
testimony to us: the blood and the ashes. The blood is at
the bottom of the altar, and the ashes are in the clean
place. The blood is proof that God's requirement has been
fully met, and now we are under God's acceptance. The
ashes declare that all our judgment is over. The ashes are
the remainder of something that has been burnt. Christ
has been burnt and thoroughly judged on our behalf. He
has passed through all the judgment, so the remainder is
ashes. When we see the ashes, we realize that the
judgment is past. Hallelujah for such a sin offering! The
blood and the ashes are very meaningful to us.

OUTSIDE THE CAMP

There is one more matter. Hebrews 13:11-12 tells us
that Jesus as the sin offering was burned outside the
camp. "For the bodies of those animals, whose blood is
brought into the Holy of Holies by the high priest
concerning sin, are burned outside the camp. Wherefore
also Jesus, that He might sanctify the people through His
own blood, suffered outside the gate." Since Jesus suffered
outside the camp, those of us who enjoy Him as the sin
offering must also be outside the gate. We must follow
Him outside of the world and any religious camp. We must
be outside of any religious organization and any kind of
worldly organization. Christ was judged there, and that
is also our place. The more we are outside the gate, the
more we are in the place where Jesus was burned into
ashes. Then we can really enjoy Him and praise Him for
the blood and the ashes. We are on the same standing
as the ashes. We are the followers of Christ who have left

the camp. We are not in any kind of worldly or religious organization. The redeeming Jesus has led us out of all these things. Now all we see is the blood and the ashes. Those who follow Jesus out of the camp also become ashes. We are nothing but ashes following Jesus. This is the full enjoyment of Christ as the sin offering.

Chapter Twenty-One

THE EXPERIENCE OF CHRIST AS OUR TRESPASS OFFERING

Scripture Reading: Lev. 5:1-19; 6:1-7; 7:7; 1 Pet. 2:24; Isa. 53:6b, 10a, 11b

THE SIN AND THE TRESPASS OFFERING

The last of the five offerings is the trespass offering. We may have a problem trying to understand the difference between the sin offering and the trespass offering. In reading Leviticus 4 and 5, many have become confused. This is because chapter five is for the trespass offering, yet the sin offering is also mentioned several times.

Let us look at some of the verses in Leviticus 5. "And he shall bring his trespass offering unto the Lord for his sin which he hath sinned, a female from the flock, a lamb or a kid of the goats, for a sin offering; and the priest shall make an atonement for him concerning his sin. And if he be not able to bring a lamb, then he shall bring for his trespass, which he hath committed, two turtledoves, or two young pigeons, unto the Lord; one for a sin offering, and the other for a burnt offering" (Lev. 5:6-7). This is a trespass offering, but part of it is for a sin offering. At the end of verse 9 it says "it is a sin offering." This means that these two offerings are closely related to one another.

Leviticus 4 speaks of the matter of doing wrong unwillingly. That needs the sin offering. Chapter five concerns the trespass offering, yet notice verses 17 and 18: "And if a soul sin, and commit any of these things which are forbidden to be done by the commandments of the

Lord; though he knew it not, yet is he guilty, and shall bear his iniquity. And he shall bring a ram without blemish out of the flock, with thy estimation, for a trespass offering, unto the priest: and the priest shall make an atonement for him concerning the thing wherein he sinned unwittingly and knew it not, and it shall be forgiven him" (lit.). Although it is speaking of the trespass offering, it is the same as the sin offering.

What is the difference between an apple tree and an apple? You may say that one is the seed and the other is the fruit. In a sense there is a difference, but in another sense there is nearly no difference. When you sow a grain of wheat into the earth, it produces many grains. The many grains are the fruit of the one grain. Eventually every grain of the fruit is the same as the seed. It is the same with the trespass offering and the sin offering. They are alike, yet there is also a difference.

NATURE AND DEEDS

First Peter 2:24 tells us that the Lord Jesus in His own self bore our sins in His own body on the tree. But 2 Corinthians 5:21 says that He was made sin for us. He was made sin for us, and He bore our sins. Sins are the trespasses, iniquities, and transgressions which we have committed. But sin is different. What then is the difference between sins and sin? Sin is in our nature, but sins are our actions and deeds. Using the illustration of the seed and the fruit, we see two aspects. The first aspect is the seed in our nature, and the second aspect is the fruit in our deeds. In other words, sin refers to our sinful nature, and sins refer to our sinful deeds. One is the nature, and the other is the deed.

We are all the same in nature, but we may vary greatly in our deeds. You may hate people, and I may love people. You may be proud, and I may be humble. You may have killed several people, and I have killed none. We are so different in our actions, but we are absolutely the same in our nature. Do you think that you are better in nature than a bank robber? Do you think that your nature is better than those who have committed the worst crimes? As far as our nature is concerned, there is no difference. Whether we are good or bad, whether we are moral or immoral, we are all identical in nature. But our deeds and actions may be very different from one another. So we have two problems: the problem of sin in our nature and the problem of sins in our actions and behavior.

Suppose a man is proud and full of hatred and that he has done much damage to his family and friends. Yet another man is very good; from the day he was born until now he has hardly done anything wrong. He is such a good person. We are all very clear that the bad one needs the blood of Jesus. Jesus died on the cross for all his sins, and when he trusts in Jesus, he appreciates His blood so much. But does the good person need the blood of the Lamb of God? The blood is for the cleansing of sins, but he seemingly does not have any sins. He is apparently so perfect and fine. Why should he need the blood of Jesus? Yet we must realize that he is only fine and perfect outwardly in the eyes of man. Inwardly he is just sin. Regardless of whether people are good or bad, inwardly everyone is terrible. We all need Jesus, because Jesus not only bears our sins, but He was also made sin for us.

SIN AND SINS

We must realize that not only have we committed sins, but we are also sin. We may have never committed anything evil, but inwardly we are sin. It does not matter whether an apple tree brings forth apples or not; it is still an apple tree. Praise the Lord! On the one hand He was made sin for us, and on the other hand He bears all of our sins. He is the sin offering, and He is also the trespass offering. Eventually the trespass offering is also a sin offering.

In all of your experiences as a Christian, how many times have you realized that the Lord Jesus was your sin offering? He is not only our trespass offering, but also our sin offering. I am afraid that many of us have never had any realization of our sin. We have only realized our sins. We have never enjoyed Christ as the offering for sin, although many times we have enjoyed Him as our offering for sins: "O Lord, I am so sinful, but You died for my sins on the cross." This is the enjoyment of the Lord as the trespass offering. But we are not only sinful; we are also sin.

A good person may have done little wrong, but he still must confess to God and apply the blood of Christ to himself. This is not for the outward trespass, but for the inward sin. It is not for what he did, but for what he is. What he is, is sin, and what he does, is sins. Jesus was made sin for us, and He also bore our sins.

SIN OFFERING MORE SERIOUS

As we go deeper with the Lord in the inner life, we will understand why the sin offering is mentioned before the trespass offering in Leviticus. This is because sin is more serious than trespasses. Sin is the seed, the root, the source. The trespasses are merely the outward fruits, and they are not as serious. The most serious thing in the eyes of God is the sin in our nature. What we are is much more serious than what we do. Hence, we need the sin offering first; then we need the trespass offering.

For the sin offering, a vigorous, young bullock was needed. But there is no bullock mentioned for the trespass offering. The strongest animal used for the trespass offering is a female sheep. This shows that there is not the need of a strong offering to deal with our trespasses. But we need a strong, vigorous bullock to deal with our sin. A weak turtledove or young pigeon is sufficient for a trespass offering, but the weakest animal mentioned for the sin offering in chapter four is a lamb. There is something even weaker used for the trespass offering: one tenth of an ephah of fine flour. It is not even a whole ephah, but one tenth of an ephah of flour. This proves that the trespass offering is not as serious as the sin offering.

At the time I was saved, I did not hear a message on sin, but on the world. I heard how Pharaoh is the king of this world, and all the people are under his dominion. Therefore, I repented of being occupied by the world. I did not at that time have much consciousness concerning my sins. I was caught by the Lord, and I told the Lord that I would give up the world for Him, but I did not repent so much for my sins. I would say that in typology I enjoyed Christ as my trespass offering as one tenth of an ephah of fine flour. Still I was saved. Perhaps when you were saved, you realized Jesus as your trespass offering as a ram. In later years, I began to enjoy the Lord Jesus as my sin offering as a young bullock. Sometimes as a priest I have made some mistakes. By these experiences I realized that there was something wrong in my nature that was more serious. I needed a strong Jesus, a young bullock, not just one tenth of an ephah of fine flour. This means that I learned to appreciate and enjoy the Lord as my sin and trespass offering much more than I did fifty years ago.

When we put all the items of Leviticus 4 and 6 together, we have the young bullock, the sheep, the goat, the lamb, the turtledove, the young pigeons, and the tenth of an ephah of fine flour. By all of these items we can see that the sin offering has the strongest items, and the trespass offering has the weakest. But regardless of how weak it is, as long as you touch it, you are saved.

We must realize that what we do is not so serious as what we are. Our outward actions are not as serious as our inward being. Our outward actions are just trespasses and iniquities, but our inward being is sin. Therefore, on the one hand the Bible tells us how Jesus was made sin for us, as in 2 Corinthians 5:21, and on the other hand several verses, such as 1 Peter 2:24, show us how Jesus bore our sins. Isaiah 53 also tells how Jesus was made a trespass offering on the cross by God to bear our iniquities, transgressions, and sins. In verse 10 of this chapter, "an offering for sin" should be "a trespass offering." Therefore, we should read this verse in this way: "Yet it pleased the Lord to bruise him; he hath put him to grief: when thou shalt make his soul a trespass offering...." This shows us that in Isaiah 53, Jesus is the trespass offering.

TWO NEEDS

By now we all should be clear that we have two needs. The first is that we must realize we are sin. Whenever we come into the presence of God, regardless of whether we have done wrong or not, we are just sin. Even if we have never done anything wrong, we still need Jesus as our sin offering. The second need is that we have many sins. We have to be right with God and right with man, and this is what Leviticus 5 and 6 tell us. But we are wrong both with God and with man; we have committed many sins. The trespass offering deals with our being wrong with God and with others. Chapter five says that if we are wrong with God, we need the trespass offering. Then chapter six says that if we are wrong with others, we also need the trespass offering.

Chapter four speaks only of a priest, the congregation, a ruler, or a common person doing something unwittingly against God. There is nothing definite in that chapter. But chapters five and six are very definite. For example, suppose an Israelite gives God only nine percent of his produce, instead of ten percent. He is wrong with God because he owes Him one percent. This is a very definite matter. It is unlike that which is mentioned in chapter four. This is because the sin in our nature is not so definite, but the sins in our actions are very definite.

MAKING RESTITUTION

When we owe anything to God, we must first offer the trespass offering and then make restitution. But when we owe anything to man, we must first make restitution and then offer the trespass offering. Also, when we make restitution both to God and to man, we must add one fifth. What does it mean to add one fifth? Five in the Bible always means responsibility. Because we did wrong, we did not bear the responsibility in the right way; therefore, we must add something. This means that we must realize more responsibility. If we owe something to others, first of all we must make restitution to restore what we owe. Then we should offer the trespass offering to God. But if we owe something to God, we must offer the trespass offering first, and then make restitution.

All of these portions of the Word show us how right we must be in the tent of meeting. We must realize that we are sin, so we need Jesus as our sin offering. Then we must be right with God in a definite way. We cannot just say that we are sinful; we must look into our daily walk to see if we owe anything to God. If we are short, then we are not right with God. This means that if we are wrong with God in anything or if we owe God anything, we must make restitution. If the Lord would enlighten us, I am afraid that we would see many things in which we are not right with God. In many instances, we owe God something—in this aspect and in that aspect. So we must apply Jesus as the trespass offering to all our shortcomings in the presence of God. And we must also be practical and make restitution.

In 1933, when I was in Shanghai, Brother Nee published a book on Leviticus 6, entitled *The Restitution of the Trespass Offering*. In this book Brother Nee said that as the Lord's people, we must be right with everyone. We should not owe anyone anything. Many of us were enlightened by that word. As we began to check our affairs, we found many things in our possession which did not belong to us. Many of us began to make restitution. Some found books that had been borrowed for many years and had never been returned. Eventually we all discovered that in many things we were not righteous. Some of us even returned large amounts of money to the government, and that became a strong testimony. This is not a legal matter, but if you would be willing to be right in everything with God and with others, then check item by item when you get home. I am afraid that you will find at least five items in which you will have to make restitution.

The principle is the same in Matthew 5:23-24: "Therefore, if you are offering your gift at the altar and there remember that your brother has anything against you, leave your gift there before the altar and go away; first be reconciled to your brother, and then come and offer your gift." Without restitution, our gift will not be acceptable to God. This is because God is righteous and just. We must be right with Him, and we must be right with others. He will not have His people to be unrighteous. However, again I say that this is not a legal matter. It is altogether a matter of His grace.

REST AND LIBERATION

When we become right with God and right with all others in a complete way, that will be a time of real rest, liberation, and enjoyment: "Hallelujah, I am right with God, and I am right with all people! What a liberation! What a rest! What a joy!" Do not think that this is a small thing. If we would realize that we are not only sinful but that we also are sin and apply Jesus both as our sin offering and trespass offering, and if we would also be made absolutely right with God and with all others, we would all be so living, so prevailing, and so released. It is a matter of getting ourselves absolutely right from within and from without. Leviticus 4, 5, and 6 are very practical for the daily walk of God's people.

Praise the Lord that He is our sin offering, and He is also our trespass offering! We must always take Him as our sin offering, and we must continually apply Him as our trespass offering for our relationship to God and to man. When we are restored, we have the release, the joy, the rest, and the peace, because sin is dealt with, and we are right with God and all others. Such a people are so victorious. This is the church. The church is such a restored, restful, peaceful, and joyful people with sin dealt with by Jesus as the sin offering and with all their trespasses dealt with by Him as the trespass offering. Now we have nothing to trouble us from within or from without. The sin within has been dealt with by Christ as the sin offering, and all our iniquities, sins, and transgressions without have been dealt with by the Lord as our trespass offering. We are absolutely released. Hallelujah! There is no more entanglement of sin, and there is no guilt from any sins. We are so right in the presence of God and of man. This will be a strong testimony to the whole universe. May we continually apply Christ as both the sin offering and the trespass offering.